THE
MIDNIGHT
EXPRESS
LETTERS

On my bunk, 1974

THE
MIDNIGHT
EXPRESS
LETTERS

FROM A
TURKISH PRISON
1970-1975

BILLY HAYES

CBP

Also by Billy Hayes:

Midnight Express
Midnight Return: Escaping Midnight Express

———————

The Midnight Express Letters: From a Turkish Prison 1970-1975
By Billy Hayes
Copyright © 2013 Billy Hayes

The people in this book are real. However, in some cases names and other identifying characteristics have been changed.

Portions of the following were previously published in *Midnight Express* © 1977 by Billy Hayes: 10-8-1970 Letter to Mom and Dad (page 7-8), 6-15-72 Letter to Norman (page 58), 4-23-74 Letter to Barbara (page 137-138), and 9/28/75 Letter to Dad (page 222-224).

Published by Curly Brains Press
3520 Overland Ave., Suite A157
Los Angeles, CA 90034
curlybrainspress@gmail.com

ISBN: 978-0-9889814-3-0

Cover design and author photo: ad@centrum.is
Interior design and layout: Lee Lewis Walsh, www.wordsplusdesign.com

To the people who I reached out to through these letters, who allowed me to express my hopes, fears, and needs, each providing unique outlets and connections to the world beyond the bars. To those still here and to those gone, I send my love and deep gratitude. I never would have made it without you.

———

AUTHOR'S NOTE

About the cover art: On my first day of freedom in Amsterdam, I wandered into the Rijksmuseum and came face up to a huge print of this painting, Van Gogh's *Prisoners Exercising*, with the blonde convict in the foreground staring out at me.

PROLOGUE

On October 7, 1970, I was arrested at the Istanbul airport with two kilos of prime Turkish hashish taped to my 23 year old body. Looking back now, the idiocy of that move is hard to understand, but it seemed like a good idea at the time. I spent the next five years in several prisons. Then through desperation, determination, blind luck, and fate, I managed to escape off an island in a rowboat one stormy night. Three days later, I swam across the Maritsa River into Greece and freedom, eventually returning home to New York. The story of my time in prison is told in the autobiography, *Midnight Express*, and its sequel, *Midnight Return*, which picks up where the first book leaves off.

While most books about prison are written from the Outside, looking in or looking back, this collection of letters is written from the Inside, in the immediacy of the moment; a lifeline of words extending out beyond the bars in a desperate search for sanity and meaning. A series of letters to my family and friends chronicle how the early bravado and naivete that led me to that precarious position dissolve beneath a weight of years and tears, as I struggle to come to grips with the madness and inner confusion. Everyone kept my letters and gave them back to me in 1975 for research in writing *Midnight Express*. Later the letters went into cardboard boxes, where they remained for 25 years. I actually put them out with the trash once before my wife made me bring them back in.

When I told this story to my attorney and friend, Michael Donaldson, he was fascinated and had me bring him a few of the old moldering letters. As he read more and more he insisted that I organize and annotate the bunch of them. It was hard to believe that anyone could care about 40-year-old letters, but Michael's advice is always good, and so I began. As I read them I immediately realized the emotional implications of this project. The words on the paper instantly sucked me back to the moment of their creation, back into that kid I used to be, sitting on the coarse blanket of my bunk with that smell in the air and those sounds in my ears. I'd have to wrench myself back to the present and clear my eyes to continue typing.

I've tried to convey these letters verbatim, as embarrassing as it sometimes is to read what I thought I knew about life, being so young and foolish. Apart from their obvious value as a cautionary tale, I leave it up to the reader to judge this collection. I only hope it provides an interesting portrait of an unusual experience and I'm grateful to have had the chance to live and survive it. That which doesn't kill us...

— Billy Hayes
  December 2012
  Los Angeles, CA

A BRIEF DESCRIPTION
of the People in These Letters

Dad got a job at Metropolitan Life Insurance Company when he was 17 and worked there, moving up the ranks, for the next 42 years—talk about steady. A man of great honesty and integrity, he was the guy everyone turned to when in need of advice. Born and raised in the Bronx, he loved his family and the New York Giants football team. Our political views were worlds apart, as I embraced the leftist, hedonistic spirit of the 60's, but I never doubted his love.

Mom didn't know much about politics and the world, but she knew people and her heart overflowed to everyone around her. My earliest memories are of her sweet voice singing Irish folk songs as I slid into sleep. The pain I caused her hollowed my heart and was the hardest part of prison.

Rob, my ever-steady brother and **Peg,** my dynamic young sister.

Rob, Mom, Peggy, and Dad, 1974

Barbara ("Lillian" in *Midnight Express*) was my beautiful high school friend, sometimes lover, and kindred spirit, who became my eyes to the world through her letters and adventures. A brilliant and sophisticated woman, she cut her long crimson fingernails down to working length, and gave up cities and society in favor of forests, mountains and open skies. An extreme athlete, she traveled alone to third world countries, raced dog sleds in Alaska, and climbed moun-

tains around the world. She was my connection to the feminine in the harsh masculine world of prison. Barbara's book, *Dangling Without a Rope*, chronicles her intrepid life.

Norman was a laughing elf with blazing eyes, who spouted Irish poetry and had women swooning with his blarney. He, Marc and I were the Three Musketeers in high school.

Marc (Dr. Muscrat) was my longtime friend—stout of stature, stout of heart, and a whirling dynamo of energy. We traveled Europe together on a motorcycle in 1965.

Bone was my college compadre in psychedelic adventures. We rode motorcycles around Spain, ran with the bulls in Pamplona, and took this photo one month before I was busted.

1970

10-8-70

Mom and Dad,

    This letter will be hard for you to read. It's hard for me to write. I'm aching inside because I know the pain it will bring you.

    I'm in some trouble. Maybe big trouble. At the moment I'm all right. I'm sitting here writing in a small locked room in jail in Istanbul. This is such a crazy place to be. I won't try to explain it all now. Just that I was arrested at the airport yesterday, attempting to board an airplane with a small amount of hashish. I've just spoken with an official of the American Consulate. They're contacting a lawyer for me. There's some chance that I could go free but maybe I could receive a few years in prison. I can't really tell what's going to happen now. I might be here for a while.

    I wish I didn't have to write and tell you all this. I know the sorrow and confusion it will cause. And the disappointment. I know you love me. But I know you're not proud of me.

    I really thought I knew what I was doing with my life. I'm not so sure now. I'd hoped to somehow get out of this quickly so that you'd never know about it. That just isn't possible.

    So now I'm in jail in Turkey, around on the other side of the world. The other side of a lot of worlds. And what can I say to you? Will "I'm sorry" make any difference now? Will it ease the pain, the shame, you must be feeling? I feel like such a fool for letting my life slip away like this. I cry to think how I'm hurting you. Forgive me.

I'll write soon,

Love,

Billy

2^d Letter   read other 1st '71

Dr. Mascrat   Tues. Oct. 20

— Haven't been able to mail the 1st Letter
until now for reasons that are so fucking unbelievable
you'll just shit when you hear them — to begin with
there was no mail coming in or going out due to the
riot — yeah man just like in the old James Cagney
prison flicks with crazed Turks running through the
corridors shooting and screaming with knives and
pistols and machine-guns! ratatatering bullets off
the walls ping-zinging ricochetting
through the bars all of us here in the Tourist section
on the floor of the john with our hearts stopped
breath held and heads up our ass praying to the
gods demons and saints of 12 collective nationalities
— Troops rushed up from the army base battling
the rioters for nearly 16 hours before they finally
had the place under control again — the prison
officials had a hasty debate and decided to remedy
the situation in 2 ways — First by hanging all
those they hadn't shot who took part in it and
second by getting to the root of the problem which
was the prisoners demands for serum and vaccinations
against now get this! the Cholera Epidemic that
is raging outside the gates of the prison —
70 people have died in the last 5 days right —
here in this section of Istanbul — it's just
fucking amazing here I am locked in a..........

10-20-70, Tuesday

Dr. Muscrat,

Haven't been able to mail the first letter until now for reasons that are so fucking unbelievable you'll just shit when you hear them—to begin with there was no mail coming in or going out due to the riot—yean, man, just like the old James Cagney prison flicks with crazed Turks running through the corridors shooting and screaming with knives and pistols and <u>machine-guns</u>! ratatatering bullets off the walls, ping-zinging, ricocheting through the bars, all of us here in the tourist section on the floor of the john with our hearts stopped, breath held and heads up our ass praying to the gods and demons and saints of 12 collective nationalities—troops rushed up from the Army base battling the rioters for nearly 16 hours before they finally had the place under control again—the prison officials had a hasty debate and decided to remedy the situation in 2 ways—first by hanging all those they hadn't shot who took part in it and second by getting to the root of the problem, which was the prisoners demands for serum and vaccinations against, <u>now get this!</u> <u>The Cholera Epidemic</u> that is raging outside the gates of the prison—70 people have died in the last 5 days, right here in this section of Istanbul—it's just fucking amazing here I am locked in a stinking Turkish prison and in the 1st 10 days I've gone through some shit I wouldn't have believed happened except in Grade B melodramas. Almost got raped by 3 insane Turks the 3d day while I was in the dungeon-like quarantine section but was saved by another Turk I had met my first day (he was busted with 16 kilos so we became simpatico)—he whips out this big shiv and the Turks scatter never to bother me again—then there's the two Danish junkies upstairs here in the Tourist part who get their shot from the guards and fix every morning—then the goddamned riot brought about by a fucking Cholera Plague—wheweeeehooooooo—I just don't believe all this shit—so last night the prison doctor comes around inoculating everybody with Cholera vaccine—using the same fucking needle on all 60 of us in here and I guess the same for all the rest of the prison, too—just too much—now I'm feeling better about Cholera but wondering if I'll get Hepatitus!

No word from my lawyer or about the trial but that's par—am waiting for replies from Bone and Archie about the money—this is the key to my possible freedom in 3-4? months—money for the lawyers, money for the lawyers to bribe people and most important, if I get the chance—<u>bail money</u>—once out on bail I follow the customary procedure and beat my ass out of Turkey—

That's all, stay tuned for the further adventures in the continuing saga of William in Wonderland or Crazy Goes Turkish—

A.I.T.I.B. *[All It Takes Is Balls—our juvenile but joyful philosophy on life, which helps explain my predicament]*

C. Razy *[Crazy is a nickname I somehow acquired at Marquette University]*

Please send to Say:
~~The Pearl (the green one)~~ (got it)
✓ The Story of O
✓ BARBARA
+ any other outstanding pornography but no pictures)
in them cause the prison rips themout

Wed.
Nov. 11
1970

Dr. MUSCAT

O.K. Finally a letter with some optimistic facts
ther than just speculation - as you know my father
is been in Istanbul the past week - he's really done
job - hired two new lawyers, paying all the fees, bringing
socks, books and new hope. I feel ashamed that
doubted him, never expected any help from him, never asked.
ut now it looks like my odds for a 2½ year sentence
ve gone up - much better than 30 years. And there's a
ight possibility for bail waiting in the wind. And there's
al of a general amnesty but the chances for this
ie about equal to that of a ruptured monkey roller
ating through a buffalo herd. I was sorry to hear
bout the blown engine on the blue Porsche and a
ttle anxious to find out about the rear end of the red
ne - though now it looks like I'll be riding a bicycle
r a few years even if I do get out of here - wooeee
e debts I suddenly have acquired -
I got a letter from Norman yesterday - seems that
Cringer Man is on his way back East again - Done
ote says he might be here this week (I guess he may
: in Ist. right now) and MaryAnn wrote - and even
a letter from my sister - it would be sooo fine to
all you people AGAIN -
But I've some interesting friends in here - the
y in the next cell is 45, lived in Tibet until the

11-11-70, Wednesday

Dr. Muskrat,

O.K. finally a letter with some optimistic facts other than just speculation—as you know, my father has been in Istanbul the past week—he's really done a job—hired two new lawyers, paying all the fees, bringing socks, books and new hope. I feel ashamed that I ever doubted him, never expected any help from him, never asked. But now it looks like my odds for a 2 ½ year sentence have gone up— much better than 30 years. And there's a slight possibility for bail wafting in the wind. And there's talk of a general amnesty but the chances for this are about equal to that of a ruptured monkey roller-skating through a buffalo herd. I was so sorry to hear about the blown engine on the blue Porsche and a little anxious to find out about the rear end of the red one *[Mark dabbled in exotic cars, and there was a red Porsche that had my name on it]*—though now it looks like I'll be riding a bicycle for a few years even if I do get out of here—wooooeeee the debts I suddenly have acquired—

I got a letter from Norman yesterday—seems that the Ginger Man is on his way back East again—Bone wrote, says he might be here this week (I guess he may be in Istanbul right now)—and Mary Ann wrote—and even a letter from my sister—it would be sooo fine to see all you people again—

But I've some interesting friends in here—the guy in the next cell is 45, lived in Tibet until the Communists pushed him out, speaks 7 languages fluently and was busted for a 20 year bounce on diamond smuggling—

Last letter I asked you for H.G. Wells *Outline of History*. If you've sent it, good, if not my father should be back contacting you on Friday—but this letter won't get there until Monday or later so why am I wasting all this ink—

I hear the radio in Milwaukee flashed the news of my fate to the people there—I guess I'm becoming famous but not in the way I intended. Anyway, I wrote a letter to the underground paper there, *Kaleidoscope*, thanking friends for their concern and giving some inside information on prison life—would be nice if they published it—would lead to my writing more to them and maybe some kind of monthly column—

I still haven't gotten any mail from you other than the 1st two frantic notes you sent back in October—so now I'm fine and financially secure and even optimistic though not overly, so how about some news on the light side—what's going on? What's the situation with you and Gerry *[his new therapist girlfriend]*? Is Norman back yet? Have you gone to homecoming in Richmond? Wow, I'm really sorry we couldn't make that scene together—would really have ripped the place up—

I wrote Schock but haven't gotten any reply. Have you heard from T.Jay? How's your polychromatic ass?

(Where did Lotte Flopnagle land when she flew over the rainbow in a balloon made from King Kong's scumbag?) Answers in next week's letter…

Please send to Sagmalcilar Prison—*The Story of O*, and any other outstanding pornography but no pictures in them cause the prison rips them out …Billy

1971

1-7-71, Thursday

Folks,

I'm writing this not knowing if you've received any of my letters for the past month—it seems the price of air mail letters went up a month ago and the Consul only notified us yesterday—so here's a brief of what's happening: the package with ear plugs, writing paper, book, towels, etc. mailed on Dec. 14th has arrived but it wasn't sent A.P.O. so I must pay 100% Customs tax ($27) so I've had the Consul send it back—Gallagher said to send packages to:

William Hayes
c/o Edward N. Gallagher
American Consulate General
A.P.O. N.Y. 09380

This way they're sent to the Consul by the Army and I don't have to pay any duty on them—I wanted what was in this one but couldn't see paying 500 lira for it when a wait of a few weeks would get it in for free—I got the book but the rest is going back. At the Post Office packages less than 5 lbs. should be mailed S.A.M. (surface air mail) (tell this to the postmaster) for a cheap rate—over 5 lbs. up to 30 lbs. should be sent P.A.L. for a cheap rate.

I still haven't seen the lawyers but Gallagher says he spoke to them and they'll be here next week—results of the 2d trial aren't too favorable but this is to be expected when the Police testify—the trial on the 22d of Jan. should dispute their testimony—much talk in the Parliament of Amnesty——we'll have to wait and see—I got a lot of mail last week—letter from Dad and one from Peggy. I wrote her over a month ago—did she get it? I liked her paper—muchas gracias, Margarita, tu hables espanol ahora, si?

I'm in good health and spirits—I thanked Ellen for her letter— she was here yesterday—she's a godsend for Ron *[fellow American prisoner and his girlfriend, Ellen]* and I, brings us things and keeps us in touch with life. McBee should be back here in a few weeks—I've had letters from Mark, Norman, friends at school, several girls I haven't spoken to in years, Jimmy Klein, and a friend from Canada who I met in Spain. Last week "The Hog Farm"—a group of traveling hippies traveling around the world making a movie, came in to visit us—they were fantastic, brought us books, newspapers, and warm smiles—the guards here were astounded to see so much hair in one place—it blew their minds.

Write and tell me what letters you've received and the date on them and when you got them—as Dad says, this mail time-drag is most confusing. No news of any other packages except this one that's on its way back—but if they weren't sent A.P.O. then I'll have to pay 100% duty when they arrive—I was angry with Gallagher for not telling us how to mail them—but he's not so concerned—

My love to all, write with some info—

Love, Billy

1-13-71

Barbara,

I've never been dead before so I don't know, but this what it feels like? All right, so I exaggerate, maybe only half-dead. And that means still half-alive, doesn't it? But it's not a half like left or right, top or bottom. More like in or out. Out out out out out out out-outoutout—if you say it ten times real fast it just sounds like some madman babbling—hmmmm. And it makes even less sense to say OUT when OUT doesn't exist anymore—just some place beyond the bars where my thoughts break away when I'm not watching them—past the bars where I don't follow because only half of me could go and I'm trying to become whole and solid and keep what I have together.

But now, IN, that's another thing altogether. IN is coming on like the hearing of a man who's lost his eyes. IN is the world that's waited just beyond the edge of the yoga I've been doing for two years now—the Yoga I've done just to keep my body fit and my senses alert to taste and touch and smell and feel everything that the world of OUT had to offer. And it had so much to offer in every variety of shape and mood and place that I probably never would have known IN existed if this place hadn't happened to me.

But it did happen, and it's happening now and since I hold life to be an experience and believe that all experiences are good because you learn from them, I'm learning from this prison.

After the first week here—a very horrible seven days—I knew I was going to come out of this place strong in ways I never was before or broken in ways I'd never be able to mend again. The question of strength is like courage—you never know if you have it until the moment of truth—and the strength in here is obviously an inner one—will, not muscle. And will power has always been my weak point. In fact, for the past two years, I didn't attempt to enforce it at all. I had no binds, no obligations, no financial (sic) and purposefully blew with whatever wind swept past carrying the female scent of life. It was a truly fantastic two years and ended with a fittingly spectacular bang—or bust would more correct.

So now I'm experiencing prison and barring an amnesty, earthquake or similar act of God, it looks like I'll remain here from anywhere between 20 months, which is likely, and 30 years, which is possible, and, in this fucked-up country, just as likely. I really get nowhere thinking about it because no one knows what's going to happen in a Turkish court. So, until they finally get around to sentencing me, I just live every day, slowly learning who I truly am, gathering together my scattered energies, trying to direct and focus them. My two methods are: writing—an external, concrete manifestation of productive activity, the quality of which is not as important as the effort involved—and meditation, internal exploration in search of the God within me. I only began meditation in here, and its effects upon me are stronger even than acid (if you can understand that metaphor in its full significance). The only thing to compare with it is love—but that kind of love was something that I lost before understanding what it was. Meditation is something I've found at a time I need it most. So every morning at 5:00 am, when it's quiet here, I rise to exercise, meditate, then write until they come around and open the cells at 8:00. Slowly, slowly things are taking form. I'm working on a short story currently, occasionally adding poems and small bits to a book which actually has little more than its title at the moment. But I have time, a lot of time, and some day it'll be finished. Needless to say, it's semi-autobiographical—"Inside the Eyes of a Clown"—and as I said before, the effort is what really matters because it's very easy to waste away in here, physically and mentally—but of course I think I can write now that I must and don't have any more distractions/rationalizations.

I've just reread this letter and realize that I haven't asked anything about you—but I think you know by all the rambling I've just laid down that I am excited to be talking to you again. I badly needed someone I could talk to who would understand. It's strange how I feel so close to you after so many years and so many different miles. I think it's the depth of time our relationship has shared. It's hard to believe you once wore a red velvet dress, and I was so proud to have you as my date to the freshman dance at St. Anthony's High School—even if my father did drive us there. And when I saw your birthday pass this year I realized that you're a Leo, and I guess our Fires have burned for a long time.

Anyway your letter tells me your knees are fucked up but your head isn't and that's the important thing—even though your knees remain as luscious as the rest of your body in my mental theater. My, my, you should see the things you do in my imagination, and I'm the director so what else would you expect.

Yeah, so write and bring me into your world. I've always liked it there. How long is your hair? What's happening at Hahvaad? *[Barb was a legal aide at Harvard]* Are your nails still long and made for back scratching? What are you reading? Do you smile when you rise in the morning?

OM,
Billy

3-1-71

Barbara,

Court today. The prosecutor asked lifetime. But the funny thing is nobody really knows how long that is—

I've been waiting to write until today because I thought it would be over and I'd be sentenced—but now that's been put off until the 19th. My lawyer says I'll be done, sentenced this day—so I remain caged in limbo. This not knowing is the worst part. I hate indecisiveness.

The Yoga I'm doing is a combination of Hatha Yoga which I learned from a book *[I had B.K.S. Iyengar's classic Light on Yoga in my shoulder bag when I was arrested]* and Raja Yoga which I experienced with someone I should have loved better. She taught me how to go within myself – to examine, to improve, to understand – but I was moving too fast then to realize what she gave me or what I lost until it was gone. But the peace I find within myself is there. You say the TM is meditating on nothing to face anything. Then I guess this is what I am doing. There's a spot where nothing and everything are one. Here I place my consciousness, my being, and I too am nothing and everything. It's the only "religion" I've ever really known to be true. I even have a prayer I begin morning and evening meditations with: "I rise to this day with joy, knowing I'm closer to the God within me, closer to controlling my subconscious, to directing my life; my being is bound by truth, expressed in action, discovered through meditation, strengthened by love. One with the All."

You don't wear make-up. Good. Make-up is only for actors and clowns. Your hair is long enough to brush my eyes and paint pictures across my dreams. I was in BC just this August when I came back to the States from Spain. It's a land the Gods would claim for their own.

Books I think might touch you as they have touched me: S.F.— *Dune* by Frank Herbert; *Stranger in a Strange Land* by Robert Heinlein; *The Master Game* by Robert S. DeRopp; *The Wind in the Willows* by Kenneth Graham. (Read it again; it's fantastic. I really feel with Mr. Toad and agree with Ratty that "there's nothing better than messing around in small boats down by the river."

I'm writing you a real letter but it will take a little time. This court has fornicated my mind. In eastern Maine there's a mountain that the brave can climb to sit at the top and catch the first magic rays of sun to touch the western hemisphere.

The Prisoner

Zenda

3-20-71

Barbara,

So simple to speak through a pen. So easy to raise my hands to the side of your face and then to hold you there—your eyes so full of love and my throat so very dry. How easy to move against you in the morning…and feel you moving back. How easy to tangle our hair and mingle our souls. So simple to speak through a pen.

But I have a funnel pen, and it vacuums many dimensions. From so many different sources and directions I'm sucking in vibrations that ring clear. Freedom's coming. I can taste it in the air I breathe. I can taste it now vibrating up through my pen. Uuuoooosssshhhhhhh! See it vibrate. So easy to write all these fucking foolish words but now that I've seen your face again I know there's something coming. *[Barbara came to Istanbul to visit me out at the prison]*

Remember in the booth. Remember looking through the glass past the reflected images of ourselves and TOUCHING. Whooooooooooooooooooeeeeeeeeeeeeeee…but don't it feel gooood to love someone strong.

Stay Strong for me Barbara
I'm Strong for you
Billy

4-22-71

Folks,

O.K. I finally have some definite news on the packages & money—Consul came today—two boxes have arrived—As you can see the writing paper, pens, Yoga book etc. are here—clothes also—sneakers, dungarees!!, socks, shirts—just fantastic—I thank you immensely—needed all that was there—

About the money—$55 arrived and deposited in my account—it seems there's a $5 tax by the Special Consular Service—so now I'm set for money and clothes, pens, earplugs, et all—

All that remains now is my court—Consul says he expects low sentence 2 ½—5 years—I'm asking for bail but that's a joke—but it doesn't matter—within a year there has to be an Amnesty granted—

My health is good—even my teeth seem to be holding well—

Got a letter from Aunt Mildred last week—wow how I'd like to see the circus, I bet it was fantastic—

Ronald is being transferred to an island prison next week—it's really great there, you can walk free in the sun, swim, etc. I'll miss him but its good for him—and then yesterday another American came in—he's 22, a Californian studying in Sweden, nice guy.

Dad, I can't imagine Peggy being more busy with friends, dates, cheerleading, etc than she was when I left—have you installed an answering service for her yet?

So now I'm just writing, exercising, and allowing this prison to become as a monastery—

Will write after the trial on the 30th,

Love,

Billy

5-7-71
8801st day of my life

Barbara,

An anniversary of sorts—I've been here 7 months today. Well, my last trial on the 30th of April wasn't—now I'm scheduled for the 31st of May. If the Turkish legal system were condensed into a ball of logic, the entire thing could hang as an inconspicuous dingleberry on the ass of a diuretic mosquito.

But I really don't give a shit. It just fucks my mind to be expecting then disappointed at a further extension of my limbo, so I concentrate on more important matters, like trying to finish the story I've been hung up on for the past two weeks.

I'm really happy you're happy. You were always one of those special people I know deserved to be happier than they were—the difference between our attitudes in HS—you thought too much; I thought too little. Yosemite, oh breathe some mountain freedom for me. God, how I hunger for nature. I hate to even touch these cold steel bars. But I figure I ripped it pretty good these past three years and now is an imposed time of work—so I work and make the time meaningful. But if I got out of here today there would be a swath of rape and chaos cut across three continents such as hasn't been seen since the days of Ghengis Khan and the Golden Horde—

What to do in September if you don't get into grad school? Yeah, there's not much to choose from—just 100 million miles of highway stretching all the way from thee to back again—just ancient forests that caress mountains whose lofty nipples strain for the sky—just the joy of waking each morning with your life like a singing bird in your hands and your hair softly tangled in the hair of someone you love—

Yeah, I certainly don't envy your problem. But until that moment of decision must be faced, there is a summer and summers are magic for those who know the words. And I'm happy because I think you've learned the words—the elvish incantations that can only be spoken by those who laugh for no reason at all.

I know the postal system in the mountains is under special strain and since I doubt that you've acquired your own messenger falcon, I don't expect much in the way of mail from you for a while. But leave some kind of trail, bread crumbs or such, because no one knows when and if I'm getting out of here. There's an amnesty in the wind and I'm still too good-looking to be in prison.

I kiss your eyes and lay my head on your heart… Billy

5-18-71

Barb

Got your letter today. I hear you haven't received mine yet. This is due to the fact that the Turks increased their postal rates 100% and we untouchables here in prison didn't hear about it until 2 weeks later—so the two letters I sent you are not flying air but rather are being carried on the back of a one-eyed gonorreha-crazed mule who stops to mount every half-ass between Istanbul and Mass. (of which there are a prodigious number, of course) with the resulting delay meaning you probably won't receive them until sometime after the revofuckinglution rips this rancid gobbler apart at the unseemly seams and stuffs it overfilling with death and atrocities. Yeah, yeah, the shit is flying and soon it will hit the fan, to stick or fly off forever. Every day, more arrests, bombings, bank robberies, murders, earthquakes, martial law, (and if I were writing the script, one fantastic Deus ex Machine's shovel-shaped hand of God cleaving down from the sky, spading this entire country over, nailing it upside down into the earth with the very same insipid spires that everyday call out for Allah to do what men are unable or unwilling to do for themselves). Vive la revolution! Let them smash down these bars and set a rifle in my eager hands—I'd stroke it like it was my own cock in a 60-mile masturbation marathon to the Greek border shooting off at anyone who stepped in front of my run from here to Freedom.

My head has come together to create one huge churning dynamo where before there were scattered pinwheels of undirected energy. I need an outlet, but the only one that exists is my writing, so I write. The results reflect the strangeness of my mind in its surrounding, i.e., my fettered body—But fuck that Maya bullshit. I think I can see where it's all at, now there just remains the never-ending attempt to get there—like climbing a mountain whose peak keeps growing at the same rate you ascend so that it continues to allude you and making love to that high breast of earth until it's stirred into a lusty frenzy, thrown off guard, and you take a screaming running blueballed leap, clamping the very topmost nipple in your grinning teeth—then you've got it. Then when it climbs, rise, you soar up with it...

OK, anyway, check out a book titled *Nightclimber* by …..White; *The Ginger Man*, J.P. Donleavy; *Been Down So Long Looks Like Up to Me*, Richard Farina.

The 31st maybe I'll get sentenced, maybe they'll smash open the prison, maybe the elves will come claim their kin…..

Te Quiero

Billy

*Yes, they read

*Porno? Ha!!

*Send me a pube

*What's 5.10?

*Free Climbing – You must do well, natural creature

6-25-71, Friday
261 days here

Marc, Norman, Tibia [Bone], and assorted young cuntlings residing
with you:

So, Bone, I got your letter—and received the letter from
Norman which had Marc's note in it—and on June 14th I received
a postcard from some winery *[Bone and his so cool Dad, Sy, were wine
importers with Spanish contacts in Bilbao through his Mom's family]* in
Calif. that had been mailed on <u>May 13th</u>.

Derish, I sure hope for Melissa's *[Marc's luscious girlfriend]* sake
that your cock hasn't become as impotent as your writing hand. 20
cents for an airmail stamp, 1 cent for an envelope—toilet paper and
2 mills worth of ink—not much for a prosperous manabouttown—
then just some happening bullshit—a quick lick—stomp the
stamp—seal it with a kiss and it's off—and I touch reality again
when it arrives in my hands—

Norman, the 'runt' was to touch your pride which it obviously
did and spur a letter out of you—the 'Shakespeare' was for your ego
and fully deserved after reading the letter you finally managed to
pen—It's really strange how you and I are of similar minds in so
many ways and yet find ourselves in such divergent circumstances so
often. I'm truly glad for our California exodus *[a wondrous cross-
country drive we made in 1968]* I play it often on the Wayback
Machine—On the High Road with the Great God Mescalito and
the noble steed Bluecephalus *[my little blue Corvair, named after
Alexander's great horse]* and a God's-Eye-shining sky—and Grand
Lake Lodge—and sunrise over the Salt Flats—-

I'm glad you're with the sea now *[Norman was working off the
Alaskan coast on a salmon boat]*. I grieve its loss but can feel it
through you and your words.

But still the divergence—now while you're riding through rainbows I'm wallowing in a sewer—and although, of course, I'll survive,
let me tell you it truly does stink here—taints the air my soul
breathes—

Yet how sweet will a flower smell in free sunlight when June 3d, 1973 drags its dawning across this wait of years and I'm out in lovely life again—

Amnesty news is scattered—several major parties asked for it last week in Parliament but the motion was rejected until the situation *[Turkey was in one its periodic upheavals]* settles—technically this could be on July 24th but perhaps they'll vote to extend the current status quo a few more months—I do think I'll be free when this present situation ends but when that will be only Allah (and maybe the Answer Man) knows—

And Ron (the spade cat in here) and I just found out our two ½ tickets in the Austrian Lottery both won back their admittance fee of $56 so we bought new ones and I had already bought another so now I have 3 tickets in Austria, one in N.Y. state if Bone isn't bullshitting me about that, a ratpie entered in Mother Mustapha's Cookery Contest, and a patent-pending for an electrified walrus dick that would put Lotte Flopnagle back pounding the meatbeat—

Did Norman jump from a plane yet? Did he reach the ground yet? Is Derish jumping? Run any Rhino Pits *[An insane college ritual performed at the Milwaukee Zoo]* lately?

Bone, as far as my parents are concerned, if you can think of anything to say, well yeah, I guess it would be good to visit them but it might be a mite heavy scene so if you want to—do it. My mother would dig seeing you and my old man thinks you're A.O.K., working steady and all. Although he believes you to be a bit strange, like all my friends, but what can he expect when you hang around with Norman and live with Marc so if the three of you wanted to hack it, it probably would do my folks some good to see you all—

And you still can't juggle four, huh? Last heard of, Maryann *[Maryann's nickname was Lusty]* was in Tunisia and a bit lonely for old friends so perhaps she's on her way home but who knows, certainly her least of all—

I don't like your word 'contact' so I'll let K's address ride for awhile *[Bone wanted to contact my old girlfriend, but they didn't call him Bone for nothing]* although she has really blown my head out—man, I just got to get out of here—

Norman, I'm ploughing through *Ulysses*, face to the wind of words, troughing the stream of consciousness, Irishing images of you in Daedalus the younger—

You dudes would be amazed at the Yoga postures I can work my body into and the astounding results obtained thereby—a Monosexualpsychic experience—

What hath man wrought with God braying donkey-voiced on the night wind and the screams of children being beaten echoing down the cold corridors? *[One of the new kids had gotten raped and the guards were extracting justice on the perpetrators]*

(If the fool would persist in his folly he would become wise…You never know what is enough unless you know what is more than enough…)

Catch ya balls in ya hands an howl in their face with laughter cuz that's all it takes…

Cooty Leeker

7-13-71

Folks,

I just don't know what's happening. I haven't heard from you in 3 weeks—and the Consul hasn't been here in longer than that. I haven't gotten the vitamin package yet since he hasn't come out—

The good things to report are: more amnesty news and rash of fruit—we haven't had fruit in 2 months and now grapes, peaches, lemons, apricots, and pears arrive—I'm fruited to the eyes—

I've got two small cavities that the dentist here is going to fix— he's a Lebanese dentist—-pretty good I think—will find out next Tuesday—

Rob wrote me a letter about the car—did he get my reply? Is he off to London yet?

And what's happening with Austria? I'm feeling really good, the summer agrees with me—we're playing volleyball all day long—

Still no news about transfer since Consul seems indifferent about visiting—I still hope to see him tomorrow or Thursday—

What's Peggy doing this summer? Beach undoubtedly—

And Rob's letter said Nana hit it big at Bingo—about time.

Dad, I told you in the last letter about not giving Yelmer *[our shifty Turkish lawyer]* any money—haven't seen any of them since the trial—

That vulture of a woman *[one of many lawyers]* was here today, I told her to keep patient—I didn't tell her for how long, which I figure to be forever—She's a leech but without teeth—I signed her away and there are no legal binds—

I received two letters from Florence *[my cousin, an almost nun, now a wonderful nurse with a couple of kids]* mailed on May1st—she sent it by regular instead of airmail so of course it took two months—I think those wild kids are addling her brain—but it was good to hear from her and I'm writing back this week—

Yeah, Mom, you really missed my hair—you'd have loved it this last month, nice and neat—but now it's growing like bleached crabgrass and is so thick after shaving that I can't even brush it—by Amnesty time I'll look like an Albino African—

Money good, body hard, mind revving up above the red line, laughing for no reason at all—

Love,
Billy

8-8-71
August Almost Over

Barbara,

I am royally smashed out of my mind from a homemade concoction of those smooth little devils nobody eats from California
because the strike, but here its ok to eat them and better to crush the
fuck out of them thereby separating body and blood and after waiting 18 days though I couldn't and waited 10 making a sacrifice upon
the altar of Bacchus where I haven't been for 11 months now—
    Your letter came this morning and shook me up in several ways.
Happiness was the first good way just to see it. But heavy heart hearing about your picking *[Barbara fell climbing a glacier in Alaska and
her ice axe stuck into her face]*—why didn't you try sticking it in the
rock as you slid. It would have stopped your fall a lot better than
your face.
    I'm glad Sir Hillary *[her surgeon was a climber who had done
Everest]* fixed your face up, but it doesn't matter so much, you'd be
beautiful anyway. What really zonked me was the day—August 2nd,
1971. Now your mother's gypsy prediction is heavy enough but that
day was a special one for me—my 300th day here and more signifi-
cant, my 8888th day of existence—I waited and meditated all day
trying to pick up influences but it all seemed just blank, but then I
read your letter and, shazaaaam, I feel those eights tumbling over
and over down that mountain…
    So anyway it's done and now's a load of experience, which is the
thing—and as for my favorite part of the letter, I've made love to you
for years. Now I'd just like to be with you away from people around
me all the fucking time in a high place where swift things fly. I'm a
grasshopper of the Misty Mountains, meadowing flower alleys in
Spring in a laughing leap, mounting mountain butterflies who wrap
me round with rainbow wings…
    My book is making me happy although it has gotten complete-
ly out of control. I have no idea what's happening but it just continues and at the moment Cooty Leeker's in the orangutan tent and the

wrestling's about to begin while Vito's just outjerked 15 drunk ploughboys in the Hootch Tent with Lulu Mae Clutchum acting as judge…

This consecration concoction has surely done its job and o how good the transubstantiation (my, what a long word) feels. When two more generations of dandelions bloom on the night fields of Seton Hall *[our high school on Long Island]* we have a touching of bodies to match the touching of minds—

Still laughing for so many reasons now

Touching you

Billy

8-10-71

Folks,

Well, the Consul finally came today—he brought a package from Aunt Mickey with much appreciated pens and books—I'll write to thank her next week—

I'll wish Dad a Happy Birthday, now—I think it's 39, isn't it? And will also recommend *The Greening of America* if you haven't read it yet. A fascinating view of the American scene. I haven't read more than 50 pages yet but it seems a most appropriate book to be reading as I listen to the news and hear about the economic crisis at home and abroad and the stepped-up fighting in Vietnam—

Mom, you mentioned Amnesty in your last letter. It is definitely coming but when is the question. The current situation here is the reason it is being delayed. We all still hope for a return to normalcy and then elections because elections bring Amnesty. If not, then I have only 21 more months and a few days—

Nana, I want to thank you for your money—it's being put to use—the dentist is doing some work on my teeth—I have two small cavities and two fillings that have come loose—Compared to the U.S. prices, the dentist here is really dirt cheap but it is still draining my funds so if you can send Nana's money it would help—

Obviously nothing yet on Austria but the big money drawing is coming up on October 1st. All we have to do is last through the 29,000 drawings in Sept. for $115.60 then hit the big prizes on Oct. 1st—40, 80 and $200,000—and even with dollar devaluation, that's still a lot of dust—

What's happening with Norman? Marc and McBee don't know where he is—what did he tell you people when he was there—is he coming here? Knowing Norman, if he sets foot in Turkey he'll probably get arrested for something so I'll have him in the next cell for company—

My Turkish friend who's in love with Peggy was just sent to another jail—he killed two people and was sentenced to 26 years—you get the good ones, Peg—

It still may be jail but it's not so bad—all experience—I still wake up smiling in the morning—

Love to all you people,

Billy

Fri. August 27th
1971

Folks,

By now I hope Marc has called to explain what he had done by telling you I was in depths of depression and locked in solitary confinement. I know he exaggerates and guess this is what he must have done to Gerry — and she, being a very sensitive person, felt she should try and do something to help.

If he hasn't called by now then I'm truly sorry because you've been worrying all this time. I wrote him the same day Dad's letter arrived. I only had 5 lira worth of stamps left and wanted him to tell you in person (or on the phone) what was happening — I don't want you to think I'm making up good news just to make you not worry — if I was in solitary being beaten every day, believe me, you'd hear about it! You and the Consul and half Turkey from my cursing screams —

No, I'm in the Tourist coach and and as usual, happy but locked —

In fact, happier than usual because I am getting alot done on my book even though for the life of me I can't get control of it, it's just running wild. Maybe that's because I'm not.) Anyway

8-29-71

Folks,

By now I hope Marc has called to explain what he has done by telling you I was in depths of depression and locked in solitary confinement. I know he exaggerates and guess this is what he must have done to Gerry *[Marc's therapist girlfriend]* and she, being a very sensitive person, felt she should try and do something to help.

If he hasn't called by now then I'm truly sorry because you've been worrying all this time. I wrote him the same day Dad's letter arrived. I only had 5 lira worth of stamps left and wanted him to tell you in person (or on the phone) what was happening—I didn't want you to think I'm making up good news just to make you not worry—if I was in solitary being beaten every day, believe me, you'd hear about it! You and the Consul and half Turkey from my cursing screams—

No, I'm in the Tourist block and as usual, happy but locked—

In fact, happier than usual because I am getting a lot done on my book even though for the life of me I can't get control of it, it's just running wild. Maybe this is because I'm not. Anyway it's fun and gives a substantial purpose to this meaningless place—

Have you read *The Greening of America* yet? If so, did you notice the 3d, 4th, and 5th lines of page 279? Regardless of what you might think about the rest of the book, remember what I've been saying all along about this situation I'm in and about life in general? Almost exact, word for word, no?

Your letter said money has been sent so I guess the Consul will bring it out next week. When I spoke to him last week he said he'd bring it when it arrived: knowing I'm broke, Erdu-Bey lent me 100 lira. So things are okay that way. I still don't think that package has arrived though.

Aunt Mickey's package contained a game called "High Q" which drove people here nuts—I can get the black one in the center though (of course).

If amnesty doesn't come before Christmas then there's always the spring—

Maybe you think I'm pulling your legs but I'm like a machine— 50 pushups, 50 situps and now 2 miles in the morning—but I'd sure like to swim.

If Marc didn't call to right things I'll cut off one of his ears when I get out—

Laughing, writing, experiencing, missing you all
Billy

9-30-71

Folks,

Well, well, the Consul brought out my money last week so that's finally settled—$95 dollars because I guess Washington must charge $5 for handling—but it's OK, thanks, I needed it.

And so tomorrow they dip into that big drum in Austria and remove 3 tickets—I see no reason why mine shouldn't be one of them.

Nothing else to report here—days continue to pass—in one week I'll be here 1 year then have only about 20 more months—no news about Amnesty but we still expect it and wait for it because there is a saying about hope springing eternal…

So Rob is expecting his interviews already—tell him not to take a Custom's job with the government.

I've read all about George Jackson at Soledad and the Attica tragedy—it might be easier to believe the official reports except for the murder of Fred Hampton in his apartment by the Chicago Police and the inquiry into the Kent State murders and the farce involved at all levels of the Mai Lai trials—as I read it now everyone is innocent except Calley and he is down to 7 years or possibly even less for the <u>tried and convicted</u> murder of 22 people—and Richard Nixon lets him stay in his bachelor apartment until the case is reviewed.

Yeah, yeah, you're probably right, Dad, I'm better off here than in an American jail. Here I can watch what's going on there without becoming involved—it's just too far away and around me is Turkey—but if there I would have to do something about a society that puts people (John Sinclair, head of the White Panther Party) in prison for <u>10 years</u> for the framed sale of one joint of grass to an undercover cop—

And did you read the President's Commission report on marijuana? And the Canadian Government study with recommendation to legalize marijuana?

But besides that I would guess I'm not eligible to vote being both removed from the country and a convict—well that's one less vote Dizzy Gillespie would have received—I heard he became an official candidate and there's no one I see as a better President.

Did Kathy *[my college love]* really show up on the 25th? I find it hard to believe. What is she doing? Is she still beautiful?

I see the draft machine is repaired and hungry for bodies again. Have they given up on me or am I still prime material? Of course I'd never allow myself to have anything to do with the beast that is the Army but it would seem as if I'm prime for them—a 24 year old, healthy, certified convict.

I must be crazy because I'm here one year now and yet happy and still waking up smiling (due to my yoga) and writing a ridiculous book, the ludicrousy of which is exceeded only by its blasphemy.

I think it can all be traced back to being dropped on my head when I was 6 months old. But Mom already knows this.

Ellen comes out to visit which is a beautifully refreshing change from all these stale faces I look at here—she's teaching English and waiting for Ronald who goes free in about 6 ½ months now.

Bone wrote and told me that Mr.McBee was mugged in NYC a while back—not hurt but quite angry and thinking about taking karate lessons—so I guess New York is still the same.

I went wild when Aunt Mickey wrote telling me about Uncle Jimmy jumping off the boat in his underwear down in Barbados.

So what else? Nana's wrist I hope is mending. Peggy's sly birthday move seems to indicate she's becoming a woman. If Amnesty comes I'll definitely let you know. If Austria comes through discreetly let me now (but refrain from notifying the IRS please).

Love to all,
Billy

10-21-71, Thursday

Folks,

I waited until the week was over to see if the Consul was coming but he didn't. In Dad's letter you spoke about a bombing which was news to us here since the Turk papers never mentioned it—anyway that's good enough reason for the Consul not to come—so I'll write when he does and let you know about Aunt Mickey's harmonica(?) and/or the books—

Enclosed, as you see, is a recent photo I found of Peggy—I recognized her immediately—congrats, Peg, I always knew you'd be famous someday with that face of yours—

Yeah, I agree about the chances for the situation Dad mentioned in his last letter to be slim—in fact there are two chances, slim and none—but might as well, you never know about this country— Only thing is don't, repeat, don't send or spend a single kurus on this new deal no matter what the lawyers may say because it isn't worth the money—and speaking of money, what final solution has been made about Yelmer and the Vulture woman?

Dean Meminger [a Marquette basketball star I used to play poker with at school] was no news to me—I told you he'd be fantastic years ago.

Mom, your letter arrived a week or two ago—was glad to hear all's O.K. with the family—I'm really sorry to have missed that wedding—I bet it was a wild affair with the Flanagans [my Irish cousins from Brooklyn, an outrageous bunch] hosting—

As far as Christmas is concerned, I only want to be out of here but it doesn't look so likely at the moment—there's still lots of rumors about Amnesty but we'll just have to wait and see—all I need is a couple of Flair pens—one or two Bics and a paperback edition of J.R.R. Tolkien's trilogy—The Simarillion—(I've read all his other books so don't send them)— The only thing is I don't know if it's been published yet so if you can't find it send a book about chess openings (I think the best is by Fred Reinfeld).

And to Nana, keep squeezing that handball and a most happy birthday—59th isn't it?

Love to Flo & Bob & Tommy and the Durkins and all... P.S. I shaved my head again because it gives me something to do, watching it grow—

Still laughing,

Billy

Nov. 2, 1971

Bone,

Well, well, well...the plot thickens. It seems I didn't get four years after all. The High Court in Ankara turned down my four year sentence, stamped it with the Big Hydraulic. But I didn't know this since my lawyers are Mongolian Idiots. So yesterday I was rudely shaken from my bed and dragged to Court again. What's going to happen now is really up for grabs. I feel like someone just shoved my ass into the Old Rhino Pit with a forty-pound weight around my balls.

But not being one for weeping and gnashing of teeth, I want you to know that it is now I.M. *[a reference from Mission Impossible]* time—for real—and for keeps. The script is good—wrote it myself with the help of a friend in here and an advisor. The only thing is what with this new Court (b.s) and the other I.M. matter just mentioned above, I need some dust. About a grand and a half, in fact. I'm writing you because I don't know if my old man could dig this program—he's always been a Lawrence Welk fan, not an I.M. fanatic. I know that this is a heavy request but so is the situation. Of course I'll pay it back as soon as possible and if I can't it will be for the best reason that exists. But in that case perhaps my corpse can be sold to the Istanbul Medical School and the lira can be sent to you. I'm writing the old man anyway asking for the same amount of bread, to be sent without any of the hassle I obviously want to avoid. Trey grand will cover all with healthy insurance but with one/and a half I'll get by nicely. So there's a good chance of you getting reimbursed at Leonardo's on State Street *[Lenny's Tavern, our Marquette University hangout in Milwaukee]* at the bash. This is why I write to you—for insurance if the old man comes across and for the needed loot if he doesn't. You're kind of like the derringer up Yancey's sleeve.

So, Pahoo, if you can come across you can wire <u>me</u> the dust <u>c/o American Consulate</u> here in <u>Istanbul</u>. You'll have to wire through your N.Y. Bank to: <u>Special Consular Service, Department of State, Washington, D.C.</u>

Marc hasn't written in a while but I just got a letter this morning and he really put his foot into it by asking if there's any way he could help. Perchance he might like a part in this melodrama. Oh me, Oh my, but the shit is definitely in the wind and it's gonna stick or fly off that old fan now...Speed is of the essence.

Willie Phelps *[Mission Impossible]*

Needless to say keep all in your hat and avoid any contact with my old man as he's getting a different script.

December 16, 1971

Barb,

Yes, your photo came. God, you are beautiful. And I haven't written. But just as there are reasons for writing, there are reasons for not writing. My reason is not the usual one of sheer irresponsibility—rather the opposite. I'm getting hot and things are really starting to boil. On Nov. 1st I found out that the High Court in Ankara turned down the Istanbul Court's decision of 4 years. Ankara demanded 30 big ones. Then on Dec. 6th I stood before the same judges again here in Istanbul. And against all hope they sentenced me to 4 years again. It was quite unexpected by me and even my bullshit lawyers. But actually we were all elated. The only problem is that the prosecutor objected again and the High Court in Ankara will definitely stamp the 4 years again. Which would mean another court. And a new panel of judges. And the certainty of at least 10-15 years if not more. So I've decided, remembering the words of that ancient Hebrew sage, Marcus Derish, "If you want a thing done right, you've got to do it yourself…" And that should be enough to give your most perceptive mind an inkling of the mental and physical activities that have kept my hand from penning you a letter.

As things stand now, it is only a matter of waiting for the necessary bread that has been promised by certain interested parties. If this scenario works according to schedule, there is the distinct possibility that I may be tasting your hot sweet buns by the time of the birthday of the husband of Martha who made the flag.

The script itself is a good one—quite a melodrama. I wrote it myself with the help of a friend and an outside adviser. We only wait now for word from my producer in New York. I expect his approval any day now. Once production and rehearsal begin there can be no stopping because of course the show must go on. It could be a standard off-Broadway type format but there are arrangements made to conduct the entire performance in the guerrilla-theatre mode. That remains to be seen.

A word on your infinity question. I had a dream. I was on a lonely beach in winter. A bottle washed up and I thought "I wish there were a jinn in that bottle." And, of course, when I pulled out the cork, there was. He said, "You have three wishes—after that you die." I thought aloud, "Wow! Heavy, I wish I hadn't wished that." He said, "You have 2 wishes." I said "Wow, I wish I hadn't wished that either." He said, "You have one wish." I said "Holy Shit! I wish I hadn't wished that!!!" He said "You have 3 wishes."

Anyway, keep your buns warm and enjoy the snow in the mountain air. And keep an eye out for one certain blond grasshopper if you perchance should wander in the Misty Mountains—hibernation season quickly draws to an end for with Spring comes life.

Will/I/Am Ha!/Yes

Dec. 26, 1971, Sunday

Marc,

This is going to be a difficult letter to write for many reasons. First let me explain a few things. 1. I received your last letter dated Oct. 28th. I was most happy to receive it, especially the last paragraph. 2. On Nov. 2d I sent a letter to Bone. It was an extremely important letter. I told him he should contact you, let you know what was happening and see if you might have any comments to make. 3. I received a reply from Bone dated Nov. 18th. In it he said he said he received my letter and was in the process of "sending out flyers" to try and arrange a gathering for the grand and a half of dust that I explained to him was the only thing between me and the great outdoors. I assumed he informed you of this. It's now 5 weeks since Bone's last letter. He said he'd be in touch soon. I wait every day for some kind of reply. I realize that this is a substantial amount of bread and that it might take a while to raise it. But even if he couldn't I expected some kind of reply. All the preparations here are held in suspension. 4. Now I receive a letter from my father saying he spoke to you on Dec. 20th and that you informed him of a lawyer who could do the trick. My father spoke to this dude. The guy quoted him a figure of 15 big ones to do the job. Man! This blew my mind. The only reason I can imagine you would talk to my old man about this is because Bone never notified you of what I have on tap here. I mean, for a grand and a half I can expect a sixty day waiting period before my man here completes his end of the contract. I know you called my old man because you're thinking about me. But the 5 weeks that I'm waiting for a reply from Bone (and I assumed from you also, figuring he contacted you) is really blowing my mind.

You must know about my court situation if you talked to the old man. The only thing is that my old man is believing what my lawyers are telling him—that the four year sentence will be approved this time by the high court in Ankara. And this is bullshit. They will stamp it again. And even my lawyer admits that if it gets stamped again by Ankara then I'll get 30 years when I have to come up before the Istanbul Court again. And even if Ankara approves the sentence that still leaves me with 19 more months here. I consider that 19 too many. A grand and a half would nullify this situation. Whether Bone has contacted you or not, I don't know. Whether he's attempted to raise the bread or not since his last letter on Nov. 18th, I don't know. I wrote him again on Dec. 7th, asking him to write immediately and let me know just what's happening. There is alternative plan B to be considered. But I want to be sure and this way is sure. But I can't tell what's going on at your end because there's been no word from Bone for 5 weeks.

On Dec. 2d I sent a letter to my old man by special courier. In his letter written Dec. 21st he made no mention of having received this letter. I can attribute a fuck-up in the postal system due to Christmas rush mail for these discrepancies—<u>but</u> letters from the States reach me in 3-4 days. Perhaps my letters aren't getting through to the States but letters from the States <u>are</u> getting through to me. So why hasn't Bone replied?

I write this to you. I don't know if you'll even receive it. If you do I'd like you to contact Bone. Find out what's happening. If he has raised the bread he also has the method of wiring it through his bank to the Special Consular Service in Washington. I don't know what else to say. I'm hung up by this waiting and it's like I'm sitting on a huge razor blade. If I sit here much longer the razor will slice through into my bowels and then the shit will really fly. I would prefer the other method. But it's getting down to it now and when ya gotta ya gotta. And I gotta.

So find out the scoop and let me know. If the bread's coming—good, send it. If it can't be raised—O.K., but let me know so I'll stop figuring it in and work on other variations.

Don't do any double-clutching with your hand on your stick,
Billy

1972

1-6-72

Folks,

Well things are certainly looking up in this exotic oriental slum. Yesterday I had several nice surprises. First the Consul came and had a load of books with him. I know some of them were from Flo since there was also a huge Christmas card from her. But I think some of the others were from Rob. I didn't see the packages themselves so I'm not sure but please thank all and everyone involved. After this bunch of books plus the ones Dad sent, I'm well supplied with reading matter.

And also with the Consul was what at first appeared to be a green-eyed, blackbearded, half-mad assistant to some wayfaring wizard but in actuality turned out to be none other than that traveling troubadour—Norman Shaw. It really blew my mind to see him standing there grinning from out behind his bushy mass of tangled beard. It's almost down to his waist! And then he gave me the Mickey Mouse watch that Peggy gave him back in New York. I was really happy to see that again. Thanks, Peg.

Norman's been working his way across Europe from Ireland. He plans to go back to Germany where he has a job lined up for 3 months, then he's heading back this way again on his way East. He wants to hitch-hike to Southeast Asia then pick up a boat for the North Coast of Australia. There's big money to be made in Australia.

Whether he makes any of it or not is another story but I'd sure like to be out on that long open road with him.

And then another very pleasant surprise in the afternoon. I picked up the result of two ballgames from the States—was most happy to hear them.

So what's new at home? I'm sorry for not writing regularly but this court thing has been on my mind. The lawyers still say Ankara will approve and I'll get 4 years, 2 months, so let's just wait and see. Right now I'm in too good a mood to worry about it.

My hair has completely grown back and for a while I thought it was going to be straight but in the past two weeks it's begun to twist in the old familiar lamb's wool pattern so I guess that's settled. But you should see the size of my mustache!

I've been receiving all your letters within 4-5 days. I think a few of mine might have been misplaced in the Christmas shuffle back there in the States. Maybe you'll receive one or two that have been in the post for a month or more.

Mom, as far as needing any clothes or such, everything's fine. Especially after that last package with the nice blue corduroy shirt. I have a new pair of heavy boots from a guy in here who just went free so I'm well-supplied with clothes. Actually it's been a very warm winter here in the big Gobbler. I hear it's the same back there.

I keep receiving letters from people in Milwaukee. And California and Hawaii and New York. All telling me about the good things that are happening and asking when I'm getting out of this mousetrap. I write back and tell them it's too nice to leave—free room, free food, good company, etc. But one of these days I'll be free and surprise them all. Lots of friends are getting married. This is something I don't feel at all bad about missing. I see from the papers that Marquette is 2nd in the nation in basketball. That's nice. Is Tommy Durkin really going back into the Army? The Air Force?

Dad, I really liked Jim Bouton's book. Especially the part about the telegrams from the Commissioner. I've become interested in baseball again. They only have room for Volleyball here but I'll see if something can't be arranged.

And what's Nana up to? She been meeting any new distinguished older gentlemen since I left?

Well, there's not much more to say. My love to the Durkins and Wizzerts. I hope everyone is feeling as good as I am at this moment.

Still Laughing

Billy

2-10-72

Hi Folks,

I know it's been a while since I've written last but time just flys by here. The days are slow but weeks and months just roll past without my even noticing.

There's not much to say. Yesterday the Consul came out, brought me a stack of writing paper and socks, underwear, and a really fine corduroy shirt. I imagine mom's A&S bill must be soaring again with the clothes you've sent here. But the shirt is really good. Winter has finally settled in here—been some pretty good snowfalls in the last 3 weeks. It's fun—we get everyone out into the courtyard for snowball fights. Some of the guards even join in but they don't stay long because we really cream them.

So I'm still waiting for some word from Ankara and amnesty talk is flying in the air again. I doubt that it will come but you never can tell.

I received a letter from Barbara. She's on her way West again for some more skiing and mountain climbing. She said she enjoyed talking with you. She says she tried to explain differences in life-styles, but I'm sure you've heard that before from me. Anyway, she's happy and I'm happy so I want you to be happy too. Even with this temporary situation I still wake up smiling so that shows something. Maybe just that I'm really as loony as the reports say—huh? And speaking of madmen, Norman's got a job in Mannheim, Germany making tractors at the John Deere Company. He really likes it and enjoys talking with the German people. Which is interesting since he doesn't speak a word of German. He'll stop off here in a few months on his way to Australia.

The enclosed photo should show you what I'm doing most of the time and give some idea of my cell. Not so bad, huh? If the light was better you'd see my moustache. And notice how strangely my hair has grown back since I shaved my head last. Also notice the chess pieces. Carved them myself from prison soap.

Love,
Billy

Sunday
May 28th
'7*

Marc,

Well, since the last letter I wrote you from the Looney Bin the shit has really flown around here. By now I hope McKee has contacted you and told you how the play closed out of Town. One of the minor characters made a most dumb move, (similiar to what happenned to T. Jay) and got his ass nailed. And I mean that they tacked his skin to the fucking wall. I missed getting reamed by the thin skin on the back of my scrotum. It was really a stupid fuck-up by him. And because of it we were sure that the play would never get to Broadway. But then 3 days ago, lo and behold, we find that the Phoenix doesn't have to rise because it was never down in the ashes. The only repercussion was that of a delay in curtain call. Right now I'm back here in the same rat-trap just pulling my pud waiting for word from our director again. There is an expected delay of a fortnight before production can begin again. But it's the old adage of the show going on and all is cool. All of the props are in place, and I mean All. But in show business, like all of Life, the gig is timing. So now we must do the patience bit.

But these dress rehersals are bread consuming

5-28-72, Sunday

Marc,

Well, since the last letter I wrote you from the Looney Bin *[referring to my escape plan B, which involved obtaining a crazy report by going to Bakirkoy Mental Hospital, Section 13 for the criminally insane]* the shit has really flown around here. By now I hope McBee has contacted you and told you how the play closed out of town. One of the minor characters made a most dumb move (similar to what happened to T. Jay) and got his ass nailed. I mean that they tacked his skin to the fucking wall. I missed getting reamed by the thin skin on the back of my scrotum. It was really a stupid fuck-up by him. And because of it we were sure that the play would never get to Broadway. But then 3 days ago, lo and behold, we find the Phoenix doesn't have to rise because it was never down in the ashes. The only repercussion was a delay in the curtain call. Right now I'm back here in the same rat-trap just pulling my pud waiting for word from our director again. But it's the old adage of the show going on and all is cool. All of the props are in place, and I mean all. But in show, like all of life, the gig is timing. So now we must do the patience bit.

But these dress rehearsals are bread consuming and as much as I dislike doing it, I have to ask you for a sponsor contribution. Between myself and my co-author we have enough to swing it but it's always better to be prepared for the unknown factor and a greased palm works wonders here like everywhere else in the world. I just don't want to hit the old man because I'm not sure he's so solvent. A half a G would be quite a grease-job here if necessary. If you and Bone could come across, do it to me c/o The Special Consular Service, Department of State, Wash., through your bank. They'll wire via the Consulate here in Gobbledom.

When we spoke last I told you how set everything was. Well, it was and so were the actors—but the small mistake is what fucks up the best laid etc...Man, it really busted my balls to see the shebang close down when we were within a goddamn cunthair. But so it goes. I wanted to cry but that never helps and now we find Lady Luck to be smiling—she's forgiven me but still had to play her little trick. This time I think the chancey old bitch will open her legs wide and when she does, Willie's gonna shoot the gap.

I'll write in 2 weeks when the word comes down and I sure hope I've heard from you by then.

A.I.T.I.B. and some room to swing them—I got the first and sure hope to have 2d soon…Willie

6-15-72

Norman,

I'm reading *Death in the Afternoon* by Hemingway. In it he speaks of the moment of truth. I expect you to receive this letter on Monday afternoon. It is the moment of truth—the time to make the clean kill and pass over the horns. Monday night is not too soon for you to don your winged sandals and gather Mercury's swiftness in your Gobbledom Flight...

With all the exercises I do here I am in need of a new pair of sneaks—the size is forty two. I think you should purchase these before meeting Mr. Franklin. I'd be most happy to see you out there with the Consul for a visit. I hope you can contact him on Tuesday and come out on Wed. or Thursday. Please bring me a Herald Tribune as I have little access to the news here. And harken, my friend, remember to bring my sneaks with Mr. Franklin's warm inner soles—this will be the first movement of the muleta with the left hand—the ploy that keeps the bull's head down before the sword slips in. Afterwards it will be a party...

My eyes await your grinning face and my feet are tingling in anticipation of the P.F. Flyers...

The Buddhists speak of an inner sole (note sp) and I firmly believe in this. But the inner sole must be glued with the intelligent hand and the substance of it all comes down to mazuma. But perhaps I speak in too metaphoric a tongue. And then I think not. I am sure you see the light and I await your presence.

Tempus fugit and so do you and your friend, I hope I remain,
Willie

[Two days later, just before returning to Istanbul to help me in my second Bakirkoy Hospital escape attempt, Norman was found stabbed to death in his hotel room in Mannheim, Germany.]

11-4-72, Saturday

Folks,

Well you won't believe it but look who's finally writing. It took so long because I was waiting for the money to arrive so I could afford the 4.50 lira for stamps. Yep, I was that broke that I couldn't even borrow any more from the people in here. My debts were really piling up. But now yesterday, the Consul showed his deceitful face and the long-awaited money came. So I've paid off my debts and bought lots of yogurt and cheese and fruit and here I am writing.

The package hasn't arrived yet but it should come in a week or two. And now there's a Protestant minister who'll be coming out to visit each week so he'll bring it along with him.

Things are about the same except for the winter coming on. There are 5 Americans here now—all for drugs so we've pretty much taken care of the volleyball competition. Still no chess players to speak of but I'll be happy enough when those new chess books show up.

Please wish Nana a most happy 69th birthday and apologize for my lateness but I've already explained the stamp problem.

And Mom, I guess I'll say a big HAPPY BIRTHDAY! to you and send my love. Your age certainly isn't as important as your health…

Spoke with Consul yesterday about Ankara but they said it's got to be soon that we hear. It will surely be a weight off my mind to have it official. With just eight months left I'll feel almost free.

Amnesty is really and truly in the wind but it'll probably come sometime next summer—most likely the day after I go free.

I guess I must apologize to everyone for not writing these past 6 months but what with the unbelievably trying times of the football game [escape plans] and then Norman's death, I just kind of folded up into myself and didn't want any contact with anyone or anything. But time passes and life goes on. I'm feeling quite good now—my teeth are quite bad but they'll hold out.

I go to have my eyes tested next week and then will get my reading glasses. My eyes are fine but an hour of reading strains them so I figure it's better to get glasses now before I have to get them.

I was really sorry to hear about Aunt Mickey. Lying hung up like that must be quite frustrating to someone with all the energy she has. I'll try to get a letter off to her this week.

Peggy must be really something by now. I look forward to taking her out to dinner when I get back (if her boyfriend allows it).

What about Rob? Is he getting married? I hope I'm out for the wedding if he is. You need some shady characters at a wedding to give it a little spice and mystery.

I'm writing to Marc and McBee and Barbara B. this week. I've really been lazy and ungrateful—they're all true friends who've written and written but I just couldn't talk to anyone for a while after Norman.

Did Flo have her baby yet? She must've by now. What's the name this time? If it's a boy I would suggest Merlin—Merlin Wizzert—kind of a nice ring. Or Wanda if it's a girl.

That's about it. Dad, I thank you so much for the money. I hope you've recovered from the hectic football season. I imagine it was as trying for you as it was on me. Now we just wait for Ankara. Positive thinking will bring a good decision. I don't want to talk about what a negative decision would mean so that can be put off until we hear.

I read that George Thompson is top scorer in the A.B.A. and keep seeing Dean's name in Knick's box scores. They're making plenty of bread and I can't wait to see them across a poker table again.

Love all,
Billy

11-4-72

Hey Barbara,

Where have I been? I mean it's been months and months and I've really been out of it. I didn't know quite how far I let myself drift until just today. After Norman died I just kind of caved in and packed it up. I didn't write to anyone and much less, couldn't write to anyone. It seemed as if his death triggered something in me—but in a way I never expected. I had to stay strong in here. I knew this from the start. And among the many ways I devised for keeping strong, none was more effective than remembering the strength of the people I loved outside. When things became too heavy I could just think of what Marc would do if he was here—and act accordingly. When my life spirit was cold and deep and my joy for living was at its ebb, I thought of Norman. When I needed the touch of a woman's mind, I read your letters.

Norman's vitality sustained me so many, many times. His dying is not something that can be understood or explained. It's done. A fact. Just the same as the fact is that he will never be dead for me other than by simply not being around somewhere, sometime. The pain of his loss is to realize that you can now no longer be caught off-guard by that grinning beard of a face coming at you when you least expect it in the most unlikely of places. In my mind he is alive. And out beyond wherever the consciousness goes, I know he's singing.

But when Norman died my physical plans for doing the New York two-step out of this place died with him. And when my plans (one of the great strength-retaining things in here) finally fell apart and I had to resign myself to spending at least one more year if not a lot more inside here—well, that's when I most needed strength and I just didn't have any. Norman was gone and I felt so hollow. Norman was gone and I was stuck here in steel and stone grayness while his body was buried beneath the German ground.

It was just too much, the collapse of my hope and the death of my friend. It laid me down really hard. So hard and so far that I didn't realize the true extent of it until just this morning.

I got up before dawn and went into my Yoga exercises. When I finished the guard had come and opened the door to the courtyard. Saturday's a free day, not many of the prisoners work, most people sleep. It's a lazy kind of morning, just like on the outside. I went out and began slowly pacing up and down in the soft stillness of a chill Fall morning.

And then it hit me with such a bursting of realization that I had to come in and write it all down for you. I mean I had forgotten about waking up to the simple joy of living every day. I looked around me and suddenly woke up from wherever I'd forced my mind to sleep. The sun was shining and I was alive and healthy and goddamned goodlooking to boot so why all the sadness? And why the hell are you ignoring the outside world? And why bitch about being here since it doesn't do any good to bitch?

So, anyway, I'm back in touch and functioning again. News items of interest include the fact that my case is supposed to come before the big review court in Ankara very soon now, today even, and if they approve the 4 year, 2 month conviction than I'll only have 8 months more. Which means around your birthday time next year I'll be shingalinging free and easy again. Also of interest is the continued talk of amnesty but as of this writing it continues to be just talk. Also of interest might be the redirection of my thoughts should the high court turn down my 4 year sentence. If the sentence is turned down then sure as shit stinks I'll get 30 years next time the court here in Istanbul gets around to seeing me. Even my lawyers, cocksuckers that they are, agree that if the 4 years isn't approved this time then the show is over. So it might be interesting to see what comes down the pipe from Ankara in the coming days. Will keep you informed.

And now you—well, what I can say is insufficient and certainly unnecessary. I mean you've really flipped me out with the earlier chapters of your saga but now this is something else—I mean, the Howling Dog Farm? in the middle of Alaska? *[Barbara spent the winter caring for 238 huskies in Willow, Alaska, at the foot of Mt. McKinley.]* Barbara, who the fuck would have believed it? Wow! To think I know the possible future freaky woman-dog-sled champ! It staggers me, really it does. *[Barbara was one of the first women to race and complete the Iditarod dogsled competition.]*

You said it in the last letter—adventures make living. I'm getting a mite tired of the present jaunt but soon the wide horizon will be there again just beckoning.

I told you before that I haven't exactly sat around on my ass these past 25 years but you are sure making a streak through adventure land. Goddamnit, Barb, how do you meet these people? And ooooowwhhhhheeeeee! if today is so full of kicks, just imagine what tomorrow holds in store. I mean, it's truly clit-tickling, ain't it?

As for myself I'm just using the time, trying to get something out of it. Haven't been writing any these past 6 months but plan to get back into it. Mostly been reading and playing chess. The chess isn't so good because there's nobody in here to give me a decent game. It's not that I'm giving Bobby Fisher any nightmares, but I do play touch chess and these dudes are all duffers. The reading is somewhat better. Been getting into Nietzsche—good god the man is powerful. You would surely tag him as a male chauvinist but that's no problem for me. It really knocks me down to find someone whose ego is even more outrageously aggressive than my own. I've just received his entire works so should be very much into him for a while.

Just 3 days until Nixon gets elected again. I didn't know. I like Richard Nixon about as much as a bleeding hemorrhoid, but I think McGovern is such a simple-minded boob that I think I would have to vote for Tricky Dick *[I'm stunned and embarrassed to read this because I despised Nixon for his hypocrisy and his anti-hippie world view]*. But that's all irrelevant when viewed along with the main issue of the campaign—i.e.—will grass become legal or not in California. If it ever passes the state will be out of control. Ah! The opportunities for a young man with smuggler inclinations!

So anyway that's my piece of mind for today—I want to hear more from you soon. Take care of yourself in the wild north, watch

out for the Nanook, don't tie your shoe around any randy huskies,
feel me feeling you in your sleep.

   Not necessarily stoned, but beautiful

   Love,

   Billy

11-20-72, Monday

Folks,

Well, the package arrived on Thursday and I'm most grateful for it. Everything I wanted and needed. I have the long underwear and sweatsuit on right now. It really keeps me warm.

Still no word from Ankara yet. I begin to get strange feelings but I attest it to nerves and so anxiously await a result. I've written to the lawyers but I doubt if that will even bring a response. The day is due though; soon I'll know. If it's approved then it should be less than eight months until I'm loose again. I can hardly believe it.

So—I've been to the dentist here and the amount of work needed is staggering. One front tooth which was broken has been pulled out and the one next to it is filed down in preparation for a cap. It will be a new white porcelain tooth connected straight into the gum without wires or junk. I like that—it will be permanent and not come out. It will also be hooked up to the capped tooth next to it. And then I'm getting 3 molars filled. The old fillings have come out and he says I'll lose the teeth unless he shores them up with gold. Also, all my cavities will be refilled where they need it. His price is 1000 lira—which is a lot of my money here but a truly fantastic price considering what it would cost outside. I have an appointment tomorrow and the false tooth and cap are supposed to be filled then.

I go on Wednesday into Istanbul for an eye test at the hospital in preparation for glasses. I've been doing a lot of Yoga Eye exercises and they've helped a great deal in relieving the strain. It's just that reading, I find, gives me a headache, so I deem it best to get these reading glasses.

I hear I'm a godfather. Well, I'm happy for this and Flo and Bob and all involved, but I still think the name should be Wanda. Anyway, I'll write to Flo this week. Also, I must get a letter off to Aunt Mickey thanking her for Christmas gift and all the letters she's sent me. I really owe her an apology for not writing sooner.

I've written and heard from Marc and McBee and several other people who probably thought I was dead after such a long silence.

It's O.K. now and I really am amazed at how withdrawn I was those past 6 months. But time changes all things, even me.

By now I guess you've been to the football game and I'm interested in how your day was. Peggy's still the campus queen, I guess. Has her boyfriend been drafted by the Giants yet?

Nixon's elected. Good. Even I would have voted for him *[cringe]*. McGovern reminded me too much of the fumbling, social-consciousness people I know who couldn't see the realities of the world for the mist of ideals before their eyes. Ah, yes, I too have done some political thinking in here.

Love to Rob and Nana and Peggy and you two and all…
Willie
P.S. California's pot vote disappoints me, though.

12-7-72, Wednesday

Barbara,

I'm here in the late night, sitting so quiet on my bed, with the lights on full but the stillness of a snoring night-prison around me like a comforting buzzing calm. Early today I began a letter to you— I couldn't finish it because I had to stop to think about what I was writing. It didn't flow smoothly, I was not able to keep a feel for what I was saying. My mind wanders back and forth with the distance that separates 7 months from 30 years. If the decision would come down from Ankara then at least this period of indecision would be over. I despise indecision—it's almost as bad as hypocrisy or Catholicism or chastity. But there's nothing I can do but wait— when ya gotta, ya gotta…

You blew me out with your last letter, of course. I could taste the hairs of my nose crinkling up sniffing the dawn-still cold. The howling dogs I hear, I know them so well—they howl in my blood, they howl to greet the day—but your dogs howl the pink sky of Alaska while my hounds prowl the caverns of my mind, baying for their freedom. Sometimes they really chew me up, scratching around at old bones of memory, unearthing things I've buried or forgotten.

Today I read your letter again two times—and the hounds started howling. They've been running all day—I love it—even mingled with the pain. They've raced my blood and now they move at a steady lope—a smooth rhythm of power and supple grace. They've covered the distance between us—they pace the snow now—a surging flow of desires beneath a frozen moon. They're coming for you and I run with them, burning to leap the animal arcing to meet your naked love.

It's so good for me to be able to touch your woman-mind. It blooms a flower of brightness and strength. I can smell the pollen of life in your words—it is such a fine thing here among the stones and steel and cold blue maleness of the place.

I wonder how far thought flys when the intensity is extreme. I wonder if you can feel the hardness of my body pressed down on yours—I wonder if your heels ever feel the tight round muscles of my ass as we meet somewhere we've never been but always should have gone—I wonder if your lips ever taste my tongue sucking searching through them—if your flowing hair has ever sensed the cradle of my hands—if your thighs have tickled to the swirling whiskers of my moustache—if you've ever kissed my cock with your mind and felt the hounds all tremble…

Night Baby
Billy

12-18-72, Monday
3 am

Barb,

What to say about being lonely in the night? I am a man—I must be a man here where men are so sorrowfully broken. I look to be strong, to wake each day and see some gain, to know that out of sorrow comes strength. But at night, in the emptiness that gnaws me and surrounds me, I want to be a child again. I want to be a wind-dancer with laughing hair who runs with the sea on the sand. I long for summer mornings and flower fields and lost loves I will not know again. I want to be a child who does not grow through the sorrows of his manhood. To cry out when I'm afraid and have someone take my hand.

But this cannot be—and I could not allow it even if it could—children taste but few of life's fruits, they are not entitled to others. A child can know a first love—a love as light as dandelions and sunshine—gone with a wind. But a child cannot know the love of a woman—for this he must become a man; and to be a man he must know himself. It's a hard thing to do, I'll tell you. All the masks have to be taken off and all the shit has to be shoveled aside—the responsibility for actions is total—the direction is vital—the spirit must grow as the will hardens—the heart must open like the mind and accept the truth even when it lashes with pain. The meaning of life becomes so much more serious—and the reason for laughter is that much more important.

It's really a strange thing that the more I learn about myself, the more amazing does the world become. The knowledge of sorrow that is so essential toward self-understanding is also a measure of your joy. I was happy before but I think I know the real meaning of happiness now. Knowing this gives me hope. But between the knowledge and the actualization lies great leagues of work and effort. It is a process of developing, of attainment. It is the reason why I cannot ever become a child again, unaware of why I am. It is the reason why I must make myself worthy of my own love—because I believe you can never love anyone more than you love yourself. To give love you must be love…

And now after reading all that I look around me and the stillness and the loneliness are still there, hovering like a shadow in a corner. But it lifts off me, doesn't press so on my chest now. Talking to you breaks the power of the lonely night. I'm a kid and I'm crying and I want your hand. But I'm a man who has learned about children who cry in the dark. So I suck it all in, take the strength out of the sorrow, store it up inside me to laugh that much more someday. And I mean to say that I do have some laughing to do. Because aside from what I been storing up, there's also the thing that I decided about Norman—which is that seeing as how he's not around then I'll just have to laugh for both of us—and you know Norman was just a laughing fool…

Night Barb
Touching you
Billy

12-26-72

Marc,

So you opened your showroom—good. And you must be working your nuts off, aside from having them milked by Melissa. But
how about a letter. I figure you received my last request. Bone is
stalling me by telling me there is no sunshine *[LSD, which was high-
ly prized by a select few Inside and, more importantly, a key element to
a truly desperate psychedelic escape plan]* in New York at this time—
come on, man, who you shitting? I didn't come down with the last
snowfall—he's just a lazy hound-fucker—try and get it together with
him—those paintings are a breath of life and joy to those in here
who anxiously await their health-giving rays.

And what's the chance of your sending over a couple of issues of
some of the various chess magazines. And of sending them soon and
flying so I can read them in a week or two. I happen to be one for-
midable cock of a chess player at this time. Been into the chessbooks
much. Am now going through an analysis of the Fisher-Spasky tour-
nament—notes by a Yugoslavian grandmaster name of Gligoric—a
most erudite apologist of the game.

No news at all from the Court scene—those fartfaces couldn't
judge the distance between their cock and the urinal much less a
courtcase—Anyway, I don't have long to wait—6 ½ months if good
sentence and a well-backed I.M. dance contest featuring the ole N.Y.
two-step if not. So what say, get it together, I'm not asking much.
One letter with a few flowers each week would be so fine because I'm
studying the history of art and am currently well into the Italian
Renaissance. The addition of your artwork would be most effica-
cious toward a greater understanding of the whole....

Billy

72

Dec. 31ˢᵗ - the last

Barbara barbara so slowly slowly we die and how quickly fly the days and here I stand somewhere between a slow death and a fast life with the gray walls of the small courtyard stark and somber around me and a crisp cloudblue winter sky rectangle-cut above my ice eyes, catching the sparks of sunshaft while my minds soar spiritward down winds of gullcry and my being rejoices in the living moment.

It just can't be bad if I'm happy while I carry more sadness than I've ever known. The pain of people past and gone, the glitter of Norman's eye in my memory, the soft touches of so many nights missed, all these things weigh on me. But the taste of life snaps clear on my tongue today and I can smell the sea beyond the edge of the horizon. I'd love to love you today. I shall. I do. I have so many times. Strange thing this love. The way in which I long to love you is the hardest now but the easiest outside. It is the easiest to come and go - it streaks the sky but does not gather together the solid earth. But there is more than this. I have a piece of you inside me - long time it's been there softly glowing like youth in my memory - but I've brought it out now, looked at it in the new light of growing and growth, added to it bit by bit as you come to me in thoughts and frozen paper images from so far away - I feel you within me - you still glow but you burn now also - an aura of shimmering, sensitive life frames you - I long to close with that to absorb it and be absorbed by it, to com in my aura of self, to come to you offeri

12-31-72
New Year's Eve

Barbara barbara so slowly slowly we die, and how quickly fly the days and here I stand somewhere between a slow death and a fast life with the gray walls of the small courtyard stark and somber around me and a crisp cloudblue winter sky rectangle-cut above my ice-eyes, catching the sparks of sunshaft, while my minds soar spiritward down winds of gullcry and my being rejoices in the living moment...

It just can't be bad if I'm happy while I carry more sadness than I've ever known. The pain of people past and gone, the glitter of Norman's eye in my memory, the soft touches of so many nights missed, all these things weigh on me. But the taste of life snaps clear on my tongue today and I can smell the sea beyond the edge of the horizon. I'd love to love you today. I shall. I do. I have so many times. Strange thing this love. The way in which I long to love you is the hardest now but the easiest outside. It is the easiest to come and go—it streaks the sky but does not gather together the solid earth. But there is more than this. I have a piece of you inside me— long time it's been there, softly glowing, like youth in my memory— but I've brought it out now, looked at it in the new light of growing and growth, added to it bit by bit as come to me in thoughts and frozen paper images from so far away—I feel you within me—you still glow but you burn now also—an aura of shimmering, sensitive life frames you—I long to close with that aura, to absorb it and be absorbed by it, to come to you in my aura of self, to come to you offering, to come to you accepting...

Last day of the year but not <u>really</u> important because we all know the little lie about time and man. But for the sake of science and semantics and social structure, I observe the custom and hope a happy new year for all—but more important and more meaningful would be the beginning, better, continuation, of an expanding series of moments of awareness and the realization that comes with each. And all these words down the crapper for a single bottle of the grape.

As you can well guess by the letters I'm posting, I have become dependant upon you. I certainly hope it doesn't freak you any to be depended upon—I mean, I don't want anything but what there is—no sense in saying or being other than what is—huh?

So mush on little husker and let me know the real scoop behind those stories I hear about the strange things done 'neath the midnight sun by the...

Touching you, are my fingers cold?

Billy

1973

1-21-73

Folks,

Long time we're waiting now, isn't it? I know about waiting but this is getting a bit trying on the old central nervous system.

Another American came up here a few weeks ago he's been in prison down in Izmir for three years now. Izmir is an exceptional prison. The facilities are new, like this Istanbul jail, but there all similarities stop. Down there, tourists are a rarity and treated especially well. Tourists have their own rooms. Food can be bought outside each day and brought into the jail. Each day a helping of milk and yogurt plus three!!! Meals are brought in for the Americans there. Four guys now in residence. Each gets bacon-eggs breakfast, packages of oatmeal, potatoes, steak!! etc. There is a library where non-working prisoners can go. What a joy compared to this barracks room set-up.

So...I've hired a lawyer to affect this transfer down to Izmir. Only one problem. To get transferred down there for the remaining months, I must first have received my approval from Ankara. I've seen this lawyer work—believe me, he does a good job. He says my case is delayed due to a backlog and the difficult "adjustment problems" of the current government. But he also says he could get my case to court, and most important, approved, with relative ease and speed. He asks payment of six thousand Turkish lira. But not one lira

75

until after completion and I'm at Izmir. And since the only way I can be transferred is for my four-year sentence to be approved, I find this arrangement trustworthy.

Perhaps you are wondering why. Easy to answer—I think our other lawyers are doing absolutely nothing. They have failed to even reply to my three letters (one to Yesil in English, two to Beyaz in Turkish). I believe it to be essential to have someone in Ankara working on this case. I have less than six months left. If the case does not come up in Ankara by then, I remain here. I do not go free until a decision is made. You may find it hard to believe that could happen. You're wrong—this is Turkey-I've seen it happen. So I've hired this guy. I want to go where I'll have a degree of privacy and liberty; and where I will be able to prepare myself for going out.

I consider this step to be a sort of compromise between the foolishness of excessive action and the equal foolishness of sitting back awaiting the vagaries of chance.

The hundred arrived. I thank you. My love to all.

Billy

2-4-73

Dad,

This will be short. Sorry for the waiting but I've wanted to have some details for you before writing. Right now I'm waiting for Tuesday, Feb.8th, when my man will be here with the results of his negotiations, the total assessment of the costs, and the schedule of events. It takes time to get all the players suited up for spring training. Marc and McBee have both written to say that if it's necessary to purchase new equipment they are willing to contribute. I won't know about this for sure until Tuesday when the manager arrives. I'd have waited until then to write but I'm sure you're anxious to know the line-up. So come Tuesday I'll write to inform you of the final line-up.

The weather here is fine and there's some snow but it looks like it's going to be a fine spring. Chances are that even though I'm in good health I might be going to the Hospital for a check-up within 2 weeks. But I'll tell you about that on Tuesday.

I know it's been a while so I'll write home on Tuesday also.

Not much more to say at the moment.

If you could, call Marc to let him know I appreciate his concern and that I'll be writing him on Tuesday also.

Practicing my hook-slide,

Willie

Tuesday
Feb. 15th
'73

Dad,

Well, there seems to be a snag in the production. Due to martial law the season has been postponed. Nothing gained but nothing lost. I don't want you to think that anything has turned sour because it hasn't. It's just like I told you in the beginning — the coach refuses to field a team if the infield is too muddy. And at the moment conditions here have turned the field to mud. So to be safe the coach says we'll have to wait for the sun to shine. This should occur when the condition mentioned in the second sentence has come to an end. Just when this will be is anyone's guess. But all is secure. No bread has changed hands and now this period can be considered as a rain-out game that shall be re-played as soon as conditions allow.

So I'm sorry to have kept you in suspense but believe me, I'm even more disappointed at this delay than you are. What remains now is just a return to normal waiting. If and when [and there's a possibility that they may soon] conditions change I

2-15-73

Dad,

Well, there seems to be a snag in the production. Due to martial law *[The Turkish Army steps into the political arena on occasion to correct what it sees to be an imbalance]* the season has been postponed. Nothing gained but nothing lost. I don't want you to think anything has turned sour because it hasn't. It's just like I told you in the beginning—the coach refuses to field a team if the infield is too muddy. And at the moment conditions here have turned the field to mud. So to be safe the coach says we'll have to wait for the sun to shine. This should occur when the condition in the second sentence has come to an end. Just when this will be is anyone's guess. But all is secure. No bread has changed hands and now this period can be considered as a rain-out game that shall be replayed as soon as conditions allow.

So I'm sorry to have kept you in suspense but believe me, I'm even more disappointed at this delay than you are. What remains now is just a return to normal waiting. If and when (and there's a possibility that they may soon) conditions change I shall write immediately.

So the light is green and the finger is ready at the soonest <u>sure moment</u> to hit the yellow alert. When that happens you'll know. The red light could be 2 weeks or several months away. By then my sentence may come back approved or an Amnesty might even arrive.

Again, sorry for the false start but we'll keep in shape for the season opener.

Still practicing my hook slide,

Will

P.S.—A question—You said J.D. wrote to thank you for your help. What help? Fill me in on this.

February 15
73

Barbara

I know of Skinner. I've just obtained a copy of Beyond Freedom and Dignity. Yet to really begin but already quite prejudiced just by the term Behaviorism.

And do you know the madness of Mr. Nietzsche? Do you hear the words Zarathustra speaks to you — and to me ;

"Lonely one, you are going the way to yourself. And your way leads past yourself and your seven devils. You will be a heretic to yourself and a witch and a soothsayer and fool and doubter and unholy one and a villain. You must wish to consume yourself in your own flame: how could you wish to become new unless you had first become ashes!

Lonely one, you are going the way of the creator you would create a god for yourself out of your seven devils.

Lonely one, you are going the way of the lover: yourself, you love, and therefore you despise yourself, as only lovers despise. The lover would create because he despises! What does he know of love who did not have to despise precisely what he loved!

Go into your loneliness with your love and with your creation, my brother; and only much later will justice limp after you.

With my tears go into your loneliness, my brother. I love him who wants to create over and beyond himself and thus perishes."

2-15-73

Barbara,

I know of Skinner. I've just obtained a copy *of Beyond Freedom and Dignity*. Yet to really begin but already quite prejudiced by the term Behaviorism.

And do you know the madness of Mr. Nietzsche? Do you hear the words Zarathustra speaks to you—and to me:

Lonely one, you are going the way to yourself. And your way leads past yourself and even your devils. You will be a heretic to yourself and a witch and a soothsayer and a fool and a doubter and unholy one and a villain. You must wish to consume yourself in your own flame: how could you wish to become new unless you had first become ashes!

Lonely one, you are going the way of the creator, you would create a god for yourself out of your seven devils.

Lonely one, you are going the way of the lover: yourself, you love, and therefore you despise yourself, as only lovers despise. The lover would create because he despises. What does he know of love who did not have to despise precisely what he loved!

Go into your loneliness with your love and with your creation, my brother; and only much later will justice limp after you.

With my tears, go into your loneliness, my brother. I love him who wants to create over and beyond himself and thus perishes.

[Thus Spoke Zarathustra]

Yes, thus spoke Zarathustra, who is none other than my old friend Mr. Nietzsche. I have deep sessions with him here. The man torments me. He inspires me. The enormity of his talent crushes me even as it lifts me up. I think of him the last years of his life—mad and shunted aside by a society which could not hold the fire of his being.

He goes on to say—"But in the man there is more of the child than in the youth, and less melancholy: he knows better how to die and how to live."

I, too, know something of dying now. A part of me died in here—a part that soared. But what remains is more solid. I'm harder now but that much more vulnerable.

For the past few months I've been reading and studying art books. I thought it would be good for my head to get away from the drabness of immediate surroundings and into the world of colour—even that of reprints on paper. They've cleared me out quite well. Moved my thinking off into regions not overly-stressed by the current environment (screw Skinner!)... And I am now at the point, still assuming to be free in July, of deciding just what to do with my life. Welllllllllllllllllllllll............

As you know, this is not the easiest and yet it is the most important of decisions. As to just who or _what_ is determining my current motives, I leave that to you and Skinner to decide—but I'm looking at architecture. I mean, really looking at it. The few books I've read make me realize that I _feel_ for buildings—I actually _know_ them. If you can dig that.

Even outside, there was this thing I had about buildings, feeling for them. Now I begin to realize the enormity of both intellectual and physical energy that goes into the construction of the places where man dwells. Architecture has the solidity, the concreteness and factuality I crave—while also possessing and _demanding_ the creativity I have boiling in my bowels.

The scope of this effort is truly staggering—as I sit here I am totally broke and more than 4 years worth of heavy study away from even beginning to realize a grip upon this thing that has so taken me.

The energy and intellect I know I possess. The strength of will to persevere I think I have gained from the years in here. The years bother me some. I am almost 26. To begin now would mean no less than 4 solid _school_ years, not to mention practical experience. I mean, I took _zero_ courses that would lead toward this.

Predictably enough, I have a mind most adept at mathematics—and so I took no courses in school.

Now I realize the potential of all that math that before just seemed wasted time. But now I possess so little of it that my ignorance amazes me. I'm re-learning Advanced Algebra and solid geometry. I'm attempting to begin a self-taught Calculus course but it is a bit much. A friend here was an engineer once in his sordid life. He is helping me to gain a start at grasping some of the technicalities. It is now a matter of 152 days before I direct my life fully again. I control it in here to the greatest degree possible; but there are bounds imposed by this shit prison scene which are impossible to break. Outside again. Outside again. Outside again. O Baby it feels so fine in my mind the ring of freedom. And the wind tastes different now when I go out alone in the yard in the early morning. And what will I discover of my experience here that will truly surprise me? I'm sure some aspect I have yet to realize will come to me only after this strange chapter of my life is finished and capable of being viewed from a perspective of objectivity. And what about the new strength I've found?—the strength of will I lacked before. And what will become of my dreams? And where will the boundaries of my life finally meet the horizon of my eyes?

And what, Sweet Barbara, about you?

Touching you

Billy

2-21-73 Friday

Dad,

Situation normal and holding. Spoke with lawyer yesterday. He said the definite decision will be finished on Tuesday, Feb. 27th. I told him I'd want the official stamped paper here in my hands before payment would be made. He agreed. He just wants the good reputation. Slowly his clientele is growing here. I spoke with the Consul yesterday. He is aware of the lawyer situation. This new vice-Consul, Gene Zajac, is one fine dude. He's the best of all I've seen. Really cares and does a good job for all of us here. I told him to expect a signed letter from me via the lawyer. He'll have delivered the tastik *[the official sentence from the High Court in Ankara]* here by then. I'm having Gene double-check with Ankara just to be sure.

If you send the money via Consular Service it should arrive in time for the completion of this lawyer's work. I really think he'll get it done. I'm counting down—144 more as of this writing.

My love to Mom and Nana and Peg and Rob et all...

I'll send a good letter when the decision comes...

Willie

2-25-73

Marc,

Just a short note to inform you that I'll soon have a residency change so if you see Miss Lucy please tell her to send my mail c/o The American Consulate here in Istanbul...

Thanks, lengthy letter to follow...

Love,

Billy

P.S. If she's already written to this address please inform me of when...

3-21-73
Spring

Folks,

The situation with the lawyers is such: the lawyer who guaranteed my tastik by Feb. 28th seems to be talking through his hat. I told him so. He says to wait. I think he hopes the tastik will arrive of its own accord and then he'll step in to claim some money. He's vastly underestimating my intelligence.

The second lawyer, mentioned in the last letter, is the best around; he's the crook who has the best record of any lawyer I've seen over these past 2 ½ years.

After I wrote to you he showed up again. He'd examined my file. He said outright it would be most expensive to bribe all the judges etc. involved in my Ankara decision. But that he could guarantee a favorable decision for 50,000 lira. The price was too much so I thanked him and told him I'd let it ride out naturally and see what would come up. I also told him that if the decision was bad, I'd hire him immediately. He's following the case, he informed me of the March 28th date.

Dad, I don't want to try to impose upon you, but if you send one Turkish lira more to Cenani or Onur or Yelmer or Uge, you're a fool. These guys have done nothing for 2 years now. They never should have received the first payment, vast as it was in the eyes of Turkish lawyer fees. If the first payment had been withheld, then you can be sure they'd have been working on Ankara all this time. They shouldn't have received anything until the case was closed and completed. But nothing can be done about that now. I <u>beg</u> you— don't send them anything. Play the game their way—<u>promise</u> what you want but don't pay anything. There is no moral reason why they should receive another penny. I've seen just how much can be done with the first sum you paid them. Let them finish the work they were paid for. <u>Don't send them more!</u>

The other lawyer, the crook, is the best there is if we need someone to separate me from 30 years. I know the situation here better than you and certainly better than anyone at the Consulate. Hang on and let it ride. We'll hear something next week.

Waiting,
Billy

4-18-73

Barb,

It's Friday morning and it's quiet, sunny. I'm on the ground in the courtyard, the cement beneath my ass still cold, not yet tuned to the thought of the sun. The rectangle sky is blue—alive with Spring and birds. 9:00 o'clock morning and a dozen or so dudes out here doing the walk—up and back. Strange place I live in here. What variety of human conditioning available for those who observe such things...

Two old ex-Nazis, an Austrian spy and a German heroin manufacturer, are marching the length of the court, chopping it into precise marked measures, spanned by their crisp precise strides. The Austrian, Harry, about 55, has been in over 6 years now. Got 12 for supposed industrial espionage. He's the chief of our block; makes the rules, expects authority for doing so; enforces the rules on those he dominates, receives the authority recognition from those who structure their feeble consciousnesses in such a manner. He's completely mad, of course.

Some of us just stand in a different place and observe. Walking slowly along the margin of the far wall, moving tall and smooth, yet deep-weighted like some massive Rhine barge, is Nick. A truly amazing cat. English, busted with a joint. The normal 20 month sentence. Changed my world, he did. *[Nick became part of the Arne character in Midnight Express.]* Opened up the colour of the sky beyond the horizons of my mind. Do you know of Gurdjieff, of Ouspensky, of the importance of just being what you are? I'm learning. I think you've found out.

Sweeping into the yard in a whirlwind of flapping robes and baggy gaudy pants, is a troupe of 15 Afghanis who arrived about a month ago. Jesus Christ you wouldn't believe this scene. Only 48 beds. All the Ghanis sleep downstairs on the floor. Their age range gaps 20-70 but they all prance and prank and squabble about, praying 5 times a day, pushing to get ahead of the soup line, squirreling away any scrap of conceivable value in bulging calico bags and mysterious pockets deep within their dirty jellabas. They're like big kids, except when you notice one ugly grinning cat with just one eye and another who's got a fucking hunk bitten out of his ear. I mean my Japanese friend has been doing their portraits at a rate of one every other day. He's an A-1 artist and his ability is even more apparent to the Ghanis. They dig us through Koji's art and we dig their strength of true being.

Unfortunately they happen to hum to high heaven and with the arrival of hot weather this place is beginning to smell like a hippo crotch...

So strange to be counting days. Even more absurd when you realize that I still don't have any official release date. Ankara sits mute—I wish hemorrhoids on the asses of all the friends, associates and progeny of my esteemed judges and limit their diet to Mexican food and Tequilla.

But where are you? You never replied to my last letter. Have you left Willow? Are you home? Is it home?

Are you still open full? Taking in all, converting the vibes to love—glowing...

Without any definite facts and contrary to Turkish tradition, I somehow still believe I shall swim in the great mother ocean—I believe I shall climb to the wind tips of huge old trees and sing my being to the sun—I believe it to be soon...

Sing.

Sing the day full of sun and swallow kites sweeping the blue sky.

Sing me against the softness of a morning when you wake.

Sing me alive and touching the vibration of existence in all its myriad, magical, absurd extensions.

Sing me I'm a God. Sing me I'm a clown.

Sing me deep within your breast and feel my happiness. Share this happiness.

Sing me and know yourself as I feel you...

Touching you

Billy

5-5-73

Marc,

You fatassed skunk-sucking sludge, I've been waiting you out for two months now—between you and that shriveled Shakespeare you couldn't get one letter together—oh when I get out of here I'm gonna kick your asses so hard your balls will fall off—

McBee just wrote from Milwaukee and I suppose you've heard about that by now—it just blows my mind to think about that place. Last court on April 30th was a dud. Now last court is May 31st—it appears that one of my three judges was sick so court was postponed a month—but regardless, if I get less than 10 years then I'll be out with the Amnesty—it has to come before New Year so get the city prepared cuz I'm going to rip it apart—I'm gonna tear thru New York opening every fire hydrant, turning every fire alarm, impregnating every virgin, invigorating every grandmother, farting, screaming, mooning, coming, reeking havoc and destruction such as hasn't been seen since Alarac and the Vandals swept through Rome...

Yesterday I shaved my head—cueballbald, as smooth as fourteen year old teat—nice and cool here in this fucking heat—

I hear Bone's moving in with you for a while—that should be shades of Ibiza *[Bone, Marc and I lived on Ibiza the summer before I got busted]*—I wonder if either of you will be able to keep your jobs, though I doubt if he has much worry about being fired—

What the fuck are you doing? Write!!
Billy

5-6-73
Sunday, Sunnyday

Folks,

Well, I sit here in the courtyard on this beautiful May morning, quiet against the far wall in the sun, amidst the hectic rustling throng of prisoners milling and laughing and responding to the fertile strength of Spring.

Haven't been writing much of late—don't feel the impetus—I know we're all waiting together, so I don't waste my time with words. Just take an awareness of the day and my being alive in it and through it.

Ankara leaves me in doubt so I put it aside in the 'Refer to Later' file.

Dad, the days shorten up on the tastik. I believe July 17th to be my tentative release date. Talking to sources here within the prison, it is reasonable to believe that if the tastik from Ankara doesn't arrive by that date, I shall not be shown to the door. But speaking to these same sources leads me to believe that a slight shuffle of papers could facilitate my mistaken emission from here. It is said to be a C.O.D. deal so I told him to go ahead when I say so. Another month of grace for Ankara and the lawyers (sic) and then it might seem a feasible alternative, No?

As for Marc and McBee, I just don't know what to say. Two months I wrote to Marc. He'd told me about moving to a new address so I sent the letter off to his home in N.B. strange as it may seem, the letter was returned to me here several weeks later, stamped "No Such Street Number". I guess I must have forgotten his right number but I mean, there's only 10 houses on the street and his family have been there over 20 years. I feel the postal system has taken a turn for the worse in my absence.

Anyway, I then wrote to McBee at his company address, but obviously he didn't receive my letter because I received a note from him last week saying as much but in slightly stronger terminology.

So, Dad, please call McBee (and Marc too if you're talking again) and inform them of my aborted attempts at communication and my feverish desire to see their goofy faces again. Have them write soon and include return addresses that are real, not some front to throw off the CIA agents who are obviously following my every move.

Peg, I love your photo. I'm sure we'll swim in the ocean together this summer. Clothes I need not. Money will be needed soon, dependent upon the Release, Amnesty, and frequency of Consulate visits (which are few lately). Mom, you won't believe my moustache.

Love all,
Billy

5-17-73, Thursday

Dad,

I hope by now you've received my letter of two weeks ago. I received your 'note'—and I agree. It was quite awhile since I wrote. I think our letters must have crossed in the mail.

Now listen to what I'm saying and keep in mind, as you yourself stated recently, that my attitude is much calmer and I'm thinking more rationally. Today I believe I have 2 months remaining if my sentence is ratified. But as of this writing, Ankara hasn't acted. What will happen if the 17th of July arrives and still no word from Ankara? Nothing. I'll just sit here and we'll have to keep waiting and hoping. O.K. I would hope you'll agree with me that the lawyers are doing nothing. What remains now is that we can hope for a decision (which seems unlikely after 18 months of waiting) or we can hope for an Amnesty.

But there is another alternative. I spoke briefly of it in my last letter. Now I want to explain more fully. There is a paper here in the prison office attached to my forms which states that my case is incomplete and that the date they have here (app. July 17th) is only temporary, subject to change according to Ankara decision. If the paper were mislaid, my record here would show that I am no longer a prisoner after 17 July. This is a basic simplification of the process but it gives you an idea. I've seen one of my friends go out 6 months before schedule by a similar mistake of paperwork.

What's happening now is that I've arranged with certain administrative people for a similar mistake. They say it can be accomplished, finished, with my release assured. I stipulated that no money until delivery. They agree.

Good. There is no chance of upsetting anyone in Ankara. There is no chance of a burn since the deal is C.O.D. What is needed is assurance by me that I can pay. I'm asking you to send 5000lira ($357) to me at the Consulate. He's been informed that I may have this amount coming. I told him to bring it out immediately for deposit on my account here in the office. This money is 100% safe here since a receipt for the money will be in the Consul's hands at the Consulate. When the deal is effected, I sign the money over. If the deal is not effected or if the tastik arrives from Ankara tomorrow all by itself, well, then I've still got the money and will need it for going out.

I want you to understand that this is another approach to the problem. It seems strange from where you sit, but it's normal proceedings here. The sooner the money arrives, the sooner the work can begin. I hope you realize that if this doesn't work I am ready to wait until October for Amnesty. It's just that I'd like to swim in the ocean this summer. Trust my judgment of the situation. I'm closer to it.

Love to Mom and all
Billy

5-28-73

Dad,

Just a short note to confirm the receipt of your two letters. Answers to questions:

1. Action is begun. Results should be known in 2-3 weeks. Confirmed.
2. C.O.D.—naturally.
3. This means clean and clear, out the door, blue book to be received. But blue book is no problem.
4. To assure two-way guarantee is not necessary. I will show the loot is posted here and then pay going out the door. They trust this since they know that I know that they play rough, if necessary. With both sides happy, I split and they collect. They've done it before, they'll be wanting to do it again with others.

I really don't see it as necessary that you come. Expenses, time, and your nerves would be needlessly taxed. All can be handled smoothly from this end. But I really appreciate the offer.

Received a letter from Bone today. Thanks for calling and the explanation. I'll be writing again next week to keep you informed and, of course, will telegram when all is completed for my exit.

Love to Mom and all and many thanks. I expect Pat out here this Thursday with loot. I'll have it arranged that he'll telegram you about the transfer to me.

Love, Soon,
Billy

7-3-73

Dad,

Received telegram and follow-up letter. Spoke with lawyer today. I informed him that you would be arriving next week. As for your end of the scene, I just don't know what to say. I realize that governmental pressure might help. I realize that Sutter is probably a most capable attorney. But this is Turkey and the minimum sentence I can receive at this point still leaves me with several years. The maximum sentence is, of course, ridiculous.

My man here says he awaits your arrival. He figures 10 days after you show the ballgame will be finished. I'll speak with you more when you're here.

About going to court on 31st July. My man _and_ Uge (relayed message through the Consul) say I should definitely not make my entrance on that stage. He says that a sentence on that day would make other matters extremely difficult. So, if we are to play ball, it should be done before the aforementioned date. This means that the sooner you arrive here, the better. I'm enclosing the lawyer's card. You'll see that he's in Court #6 at the Justice Building each day until 2:00 p.m. This Court, #6, also happens to be my court. If you can arrive on a Fri. or Sat. or can't come out to see me first, perhaps you can contact him. He can come out here any day and can bring you along. But it's better if I speak with you first before you speak with him.

I think he's our best bet. You can judge him yourself when you come.

The guy has a lot of money. He has a reputation, he doesn't need to make a name for himself. He does the best work for those he likes. It sounds strange but it's true. He likes me so I feel confident he'll do a good job. When you arrive, after you speak with him, you should stick with him 24 hours a day, if possible. Eat meals with him and keep abreast of what he's doing. With you here, constantly with him, he'll really push to get it done.

O.K. enough said. I realize you must get things together over there but the sooner you come, the better. Also, I don't think it wise at all to mention Sutter or let my man know he's here. Definitely don't let my man think that anyone (Consul, etc) else is in on the game plan. As I said, he's clever and discreet. He wouldn't want any strings attached or any supervision by another lawyer. Just show him that you're here to play it straight and trust him and he'll come across. Of course, C.O.D. is the word.

Love to Mom and all—soon—Billy

7-14-73

Folks

Well, now that I sit down to it, I find it's not so easy to tell about my time here. The changes I've undergone in the past 3 years and the truths I've learned about myself all tend to still my hand from writing. I've come to the point where my former self, the one so strangely presented to me by your newspaper article *[Newsday wrote extensive articles about my situation]*, is a fading character in some surrealistic novel. The views this character held on life seem less certain now. The perspective he had of himself seems almost absurd. Three years ago I would have leapt at a chance to pour my ego all over your paper. Now I realize that before a man attempts to express himself in so solid a form as writing, he should be aware of just who and what he really is. I've only begun to learn these really important things so I feel a reluctance, almost an unwillingness, to expose the calm I'm building within me to the eye of so many people.

Perhaps this is all a bit melodramatic. What I mean is that I'm not at all sure of myself regarding so many points that before used to be so secure. But as a balance, I've learned some simple truths about just living life every day—truths that could never have been realized at the frenzied pace I formerly lived. It took prison to slow me down to a frequency where I could begin ...*[missing]*...It has allowed for much reflection, much image examination.

I should try to explain right off that the Turkish prison system differs in one very essential respect from what I know of the American system. I believe it to be the basic philosophy involved. "Ceza Evi" means house of punishment. That's all this place is— clearly, simply, a place that punishes those who break one of the mores of this society. Break a law, go to jail. Do your time, go free. Simple. The punishment is being locked away from the world.

There is no purposeful psychological element involved. There is no attempt to strip and break and then feebly repair a man. Life goes on in here—a little harsher, a bit less colorful than on the Outside, but it goes on. Inmates, my friends, wear their own clothes, retain their own personalities, read books, play music, do nothing, do something, masturbate, meditate, do their thing whatever it may be. Morning and evening bring the opening and locking of the yard door. Noon and 5pm bring the food. Each evening there is a head count. Occasionally the guards come in for a search. Finish. We are free to live out our day as we please.

Except for a few, the guardians are pleasant enough dudes. Their pay and education are minimal, their attitude towards the prisoners, especially the foreigners or the wealthy, is a mixture of interest and envy. The bas guardians (the chief guards) have a much greater responsibility than the door wardens so their attitude is a shade more formal and less friendly.

Yet we seldom see them in our block. We are left to decide our own social rules and to solve our own problems before bringing them outside the block to the authorities.

The atmosphere is relatively free of hostility. So free that it struck me as strange when I first arrived. There are arguments, of course, hassles and all the normal emotional outbursts expected among any group of 50 men of varied nationalities forced to live in such close conditions. But there is none of the heavy brooding tension, the air of hate and anger that I expected. There is crying—I listen at night sometimes to people releasing in their sleep the sorrow that they held during the day. But the sound of laughter is strong.

Perhaps because we are foreigners here, we receive better treatment. Certainly the fact that over half the guys here are in their 20's and in for hash smoking or smuggling has something to do with it. They're calmer, more capable of... *[missing]*... and this is an important factor in producing an atmosphere of relative stability, this lack of strict, disciplinary, psychological pressure. No petty, personal, de-personalizing rules of attire, little interference by the guards into our daily routine of life, no attempts to remold our characters except that which each man wants or is capable of doing himself.

The physical surroundings are easy to write about:

Our cellblock is just one of many rectangular branches perpendicular to a central corridor. In between blocks is a small cement courtyard bordered by the corridor at one end and the great grey wall at the other. Each block consists of two long rectangular rooms, one above the other. In our *kogus*, there are 24 double beds on the top floor. They're metal-framed, wood-slatted, and bolted into the floor and ceiling. It could be an Army barracks or a youth hostel. Downstairs the room is empty except for 6 long tables with twelve wood-iron benches beside them. (We're lucky. In some other blocks the upstairs <u>and</u> downstairs are filled with beds—often with people sleeping on the floor.) The stairway partition divides both upper and lower stories, creating a small kitchen of sorts below and our 2-stall bathroom above. The side of the block facing the courtyard is lined both upstairs and down with large glass windows—barred, of course. This makes for much light and air. A bit too much in the winter, but you have to take what you get.

As I sit here on my upper bunk against the wall, it's 7:00 p.m. and the courtyard is still open. When I look out the windows to my left, directly across from me is the mirror image of this block, only it's occupied by Turkish children. Age range perhaps 10-16. We share the same courtyard together and even now there is a soccer game in progress. The noise is incredible, echoing back and forth in the narrow confined space. But I guess if you live in N.Y.C., it wouldn't faze you at all.

This has been standard prison policy since I've been here. The tourists and the kids always share the same yard. I guess this profits both groups since the kids present no physical threats to us and we, being relatively well-off economically, help out the kids. They're also quite a gas to have around. Quite clever little street urchins locked up for charges ranging from pickpocket and horse-thief to rape and murder.

Yeah. 10,11,12 year old killers. Heavy.

The Turks dig music themselves so we're allowed guitars and flutes and drums. Some evenings downstairs you could find a British guy with a 20 month sentence playing guitar with a smiling Swede who looks like a skinny smiling elf. A young Frenchman on bass guitar just got sentenced to 25 years. Our Japanese artist runs jazzy guitar riffs in the background. He's been in 4 ½ years now. Was busted with the Swedish elf for sale of 100 grams of hash. They got 12 ½ years each.

Anyway, I've got to sleep and try to grab a bath. Which is easier said than done here. If anyone's interested, I'll continue later. Folks, you said to write something about my time here so I am. Let me know if this is what you had in mind. I'm feeling good and expect the best. My teeth are not hurting but that doesn't mean they're not quietly decaying. That cough doesn't go away but it doesn't seem to be getting much worse. I have a fever now and then but it's probably just my energy release valve because it goes away.

I miss you all. I send a smile...

Love,

Billy

7-19-73, Thursday

Barbara,

Your letter arrived yesterday. The others also made it here. Writing back was difficult as you seldom present a stable target. You're moving again, aren't you? People and places going by faster after the settled time in the frozen North. It's a fine thing—moving. Keeps you loose and raw alive. Allows your ideas, ideals, to gather and gain shape—hones you down with experience—makes you solid where you should be—strong for the time when you find the place where you'll make your peace. For the time when you focus and do your real work.

If I leave here soon, I'll be moving a bit. So many things I still must see. Other more important things I have to find. But if I must stay a few more years then perhaps there'll be no need for moving. I already know where all that I seek lies. I'm just not strong enough or wise enough to bring it out by myself. I need the guidance of someone who knows and the strength of someone who cares. Stay or leave, here or there—always here and now.

I didn't know your friends *[Several of her friends were killed in a climbing accident]* but I know that they were your friends, so their loss is felt. And I know you so the pain touches me. It's part of things, pain. Words don't say much about it, maybe just remind you of the balance—'...and from the selfsame well whence flows your sorrow, so springs your joy...' *[Khalil Gibran]*

My father is here in Istanbul. Been here a week now and plans on 2-3 more. Lawyer work and coordination of politics and publicity. He's a fine, courageous man. I hope the efforts he's putting forth will not be in vain. For his sake as much as my own. I love him much.

You asked about my sex life. For the first and second year I could speak to you of strange frustrations and aberrations, of dreams and sweat soaked mornings, of sperm in toilets and wasted energy. For the past year or so I've been celibate. Hard to believe, even harder to accomplish. But I do fairly well. An important part of the work. Building something solid, channeling energy. Difficult under these conditions, but then life is easy only for those who set themselves an easy goal.

The publicity back in the States is really quite something. I've been receiving letters from all over the country…Some strange but all wishing well. My friends even flew a plane along the beach with a huge banner urging people to write their Congressman. And my family on TV and newsman reading excerpts of my letters out to millions of viewers. I mean, really…

The editor of *Newsday* requests samples of any stories I've done. I would have jumped at such an opportunity a year ago. But now I realize that anything I've written is just ego-trash. I've turned my energy in, am trying to conserve and concentrate it. I'm not ready to write yet. Five years, ten years, maybe more. But not now…

And yet the publicity may be helpful so I send them small pieces of thought, toned down to daily paper speed, of course. So freaky. This whole jail scene. Three years now I'm a character in some weird story and suddenly I read my own words in newspapers, see my H.S. graduation photo on the front page. The character in the story has actually begun to write some of the dialogue. Mixtures of omniscient authors. Ridiculous. Reality. If I could truly gain control of the situation I'd write in much more nature—trees and ocean and open sky, flowers breathing sunshine, butterflys and misty mountains. And, of course, I'd find you among the mountains. If I could write the story.

I like your story much better. With the loss of your friends it might seem offensive to say I send you smiles and happy vibes—but I do. Death is part of life as life is part of death. Chickens and eggs round and round…

I know Chamonix—so beautiful. Had a motorcycle beneath me and wind in my hair then. I'm there in your eyes now.

Love
Billy

September 10, 1973. The High
Court in Ankara rejects my initial 4
year sentence and re-sentences me to
life in prison, which my original
judge, sympathetic to the situation,
lowers to 30 years. Dad is with me.

11-2-73, Friday

Dad,

A friend of mine goes free tomorrow. He's mailing this for me from Outside so we have a bit of leeway in conversation.

Well, the 19th of October has come and gone. The Amnesty proposals are still being passed around and the government is still in pieces. A coalition is being attempted but I think it will take some time before the asses in the Turkish Parliament will ever get together. I received a formal but polite note from Amb. Macomber *[the American Ambassador in Ankara]* in reply to my letter. At this point I don't know what, if anything, is being done by either officials here in Turkey or by people back home. Excuse my pessimism, but I'm beginning to believe that the only way out will be in accordance with the adage that God helps those who help themselves.

So let me ask some questions:

1. Are there any <u>definite</u> plans in operative readiness? I'm speaking of the old ballgame again. I believe the season will soon be upon us.

2. What are the officials doing? I hear nothing but if they are going to eventually do something then there must be something definite started by now.

3. What's B.G. and his friend Mr. Ness up to? *[more plotters]*

4. How long do you think we should wait before doing something besides waiting?

I realize that the next few weeks should bring some results from the Government. And that the Amnesty <u>should</u> come. But from the propositions so far submitted, even the best Amnesty offered will still leave me with 7 more years.

I'm writing this letter to begin to put our thinking on the outside track again. No, I haven't been in touch with "Shoddy" *[one of the jackal-pack lawyers baying at the herd of prisoners]*. But I've been doing a lot of thinking and talking… If Amnesty comes and I'm still here, well, then I guess we have no choice but to try Ness or Shoddy or someone like this *[the Amnesty would still leave me more prison and the lawyers were offering some administrative/paperwork shell-game to get me accidentally freed with everyone else—if the Amnesty came].* But if it doesn't come at all then my American friend and I have some plans formulated. He's been here 4 ½ years now, speaks fluent Turk and has been in Izmir for his first 3 years. An Amnesty would free him, only 2 ½ years remaining on a 10 year sentence. He's gathered about 2 G's together. If Amnesty doesn't come we have worked out a plan. It involves a transfer and some bribes. I'll be needing about 3 G's for my end. We're still in the talk stages but are preparing for eventualities...

I don't want you to get the impression that a panic is forming. Quite the contrary. We both know that this thing must be done right. Both of us (and my friend) know what it means to have to depend upon lawyers. They are not dependable. We can do better on our own. Money is the problem.

I'm writing all this to tell you that if the Amnesty doesn't come, I think it better for my friend and me to attempt to find our own way rather than put trust and money in the hands of a lawyer.

Perhaps you remember a request of mine for a few hundred about a month ago. This was for the purchase of certain equipment which could be most valuable should the ballgame begin in earnest. My friend has possession of this equipment now.

I'm waiting for Consul to come out, I hope next week, with some news. I'm waiting for the government to get their Amnesty together. I'm waiting for the Ambassador. But I think it's time to be thinking of the ballgame again.

Please write advising me of the situation. What are your plans? I'm sure you are waiting for the <u>official</u> results but if they are all nil, then what? That's why I'm writing now. To prepare us for the eventuality of a New York Two-Step.

So that's it. I couldn't believe all the articles you sent. Never knew there had been that much publicity. And now that you're a TV personality, do you walk around in dark shades, incognito? *[Once my sentence was changed to 30 years my Dad, who'd been reluctant earlier, agreed with Mike Griffith, my American lawyer, to pull out the stops and get as much PR as possible in an attempt to help promote the ongoing negotiations for a prisoner exchange treaty.]*

Mom, I wish you a happy birthday. I can send you only what you have, my love, all of it. It's beginning to get cold here, the air is clean and clear and refreshing after the long summer. My love to Peg and Rob and Nana and all…

Still smiling,

Billy

p.s. Don't publish this letter.

11-11-73, Monday

Folks and all,

Overcast this morning, 7:00am. The sounds of sleeping men around me. I'm late today. Off schedule. Sleep has been erratic the past 3 weeks. Quiet, I slip out of bed, drop softly to the stone floor. Make my way downstairs to spread a blanket, do some Yoga, start the day.

You know about the downstairs room—empty but for the tables and benches. In one corner, just past the stairwell, a small gas cooking-stove is set up on a table. Low, thin, and metal-white with two burners. 15 or 20 small curved, vase-like tea glasses rest beside it. Cay, Turkish tea, is being made in old aluminum pots. The staple drink here. A glass costs 25 kurus—about 2 cents. Coffee is also available for those who drink such stuff.

We cook our food on this stove. Heat soups, fry eggs, brown up onions and peppers and garlic to add to the macaroni. No one's down here now except the cay-gee. It's quiet. Muffled air. Gray day. The room echoes hollow the sound of my sandaled footsteps. Soon people will begin to stir. Breakfasts will begin. The smell of olive oil and the splutter of eggs in a pan. Always makes me think of Spain, the smell of olive oil. Far away now, Spain.

But Patrice comes down with his small stool and his lesson books and begins to play....Has almost seven more years to practice...

10:00 am—A shout from the door—Gasti! The newspaper man is here. He comes around every day selling the locals. Several people hurry over to buy 2 or 3 different issues. More crowding around them. Everyone looks for AF—Amnesty. Every day they look for AF but it's always coming tomorrow. Been coming tomorrow for at least 3 years now. Good for newspaper sales, though.

Out for a walk in the yard. Light drizzle beginning to fall. The sky is sagging today. Clouds are low, a gray roof of mist just above the wall. A seagull moving silently across the sky, damp and alone, heading inland. I remember the ocean in the morning in the fog...

Against the wall, looking up past the corner wall at the opposite end, I can see the top of the prison mosque. It rises up grey stone against grey sky—a tall cylinder tapering to a cone, topped off with the gold ornamental crescent moon of Islam. The Hoja sings his prayer of praise from off a small room at the top. His voice echoes down across the prison yards, out into the city to mingle with the songs from other mosques. Muslim priests in minarets—lighthouse-keepers of God…

4:00 pm—Slow day. Rain dripping. Most people quiet, reading, sleeping. It's Monday and the weekend post is expected. Big event, the post. Nice when it comes but a let-down if you wait for nothing. That's why I don't wait anymore. Waiting for things is a drag is a drag. Just be here now and all those things you wait for will arrive— even the day the door opens. The wet weather is tough on my cough. I could handle some mountain fields filled with butterflies. A fine bottle of red wine wouldn't do me half-bad either.

A long time ago we used to get milk but we don't anymore. I still have the empty bottles though. Filled them up with water and stuck an onion in the top of each. Nice to see some green growing as the fresh shoots push their way up. Nice to get green onions when they've reached their time. You won't believe it but I can actually cook now. Not just peanut-butter and jelly either. And if I told you I can sew it might be too much so I won't.

I'm tired. Hope all is well with everyone.

Love, of course,

Billy

11-16-73

Marc,

Forgive me, friend, but time moves at a different pace here. Days come and go like shadows crossing the face of the sun. I've been waiting to write, waiting to have some kind of definite news. Alas, there is nothing to report other than speculative bullshit. Seems like an Amnesty should be coming one of these days. May affect me, then again, may not. Thirty minus 10 or 15 is still 20 or so years. Perhaps all this phenomenal publicity will result in a form of special pardon. Perhaps I'll be transferred back to the States. Perhaps...

As for me, all is well. A bit older, you grow or you die, no choice. A few less teeth, a bit more wisdom. Just living. Been writing, sending stuff off to *Newsday* and some radio, out of Washington. Winter is approaching. It's cold now mornings when I rise. 5 am and before the dawn. Still and precious silence in the early hours before the prison wakes...

I've been looking at the extension of the present situation and it looks as if there will have to be some difficult, irrevocable step taken if all the possible solutions do not materialize. More on that to follow...

A.I.T.I.B.
Billy

11-20-73

Barbara,

Hey, baby, hold on! You know about loneliness and about loving. You know what to expect from people by now. You know that no matter what you give it just isn't enough for some people and too much for others. Of course you're going to make people feel inferior, simply because they are. It's just the way things are and the pain you have to bear. I mean, if by being true to yourself you evoke these responses in the people around you, is there something lacking in you—or in them? And if you are true to yourself, giving, giving, giving your love, does it really matter that these people can't understand you, can't feel you? Yeah, of course, it matters. But could you be untrue to yourself because of it? I mean, would you try to be other than what you are? Dig, Barb, I know what loneliness is. I have friends all over the world and people sign their letters with love. But I know loneliness, believe me. In my short life I've found many women I wanted but only wanted one woman I found. And she's been gone a long time now. I made her go. She wanted more than I thought I was capable of giving. She wanted me but she wanted me to come together, to be real. She gave and gave and I just kept taking. She wanted a man while I was just a hungry little boy. She tried to make me conscious of my failings but back then there wasn't anyone or anything that could touch through the image I'd created around myself. I understand you now because I've come to understand her. A woman, a man, must reflect the true image of the people around them. In your eyes people see themselves for what they really are. If the reflection scares them, are you obliged to see a different reality? <u>Are you obliged to sponsor their illusions?</u> Hellll, No! Kiss pretty little Beth *[a girlfriend she biked with around Europe]* on the forehead for me and tell her to shut the fuck up. What is this inferiority inadequacy crap? I mean, we are what we are. The extra trappings of looks or ability are minor if perspective is held. The task is to realize the God within us. Our purpose for being is simply to love. Even if you think it isn't working you must keep trying with other people. Do you think that even the slightest vibration of your love is wasted? <u>If you expect nothing in return, eventually you receive everything</u>.

Whoooooeeee—listen to me shooting the shit.

As for letters—I wrote you at the Dig in England *[an archeology dig she worked on as part of her bicycle tour around Europe]*, mailed out on October 26th. I'm sorry you didn't receive it, not for the content but for the contact. I know how good it feels to get your letters, to hold your words in my hands, to touch the paper and know it's been close to you. Whatever developments I mentioned in that letter are still the same now. Seems like Washington people are waiting to see what the Turks will do about the Amnesty…and the Turks won't do anything until they form a government and find some kind of badly needed political stability… And I'm beginning to think that Religion will be the final solution. I mean that God helps those who help themselves, No? Anyway, when I know something definite I'll write you. Be sure to keep me informed of travel and places I can send letters.

Ah yes, your bicycling descriptions so turn me on. The wind coming down out the mountains and oceans of clouds rumbling overhead. I rode Barcelona to Munich one early Spring on my motorcycle. It rained continuously, only letting up for an occasional snowstorm. I mean to say that I almost literally froze my nuts off. Took me twelve days and I even now consider it one of the most strenuous mental and physical experiences I've ever had. So I could feel that hot shower you spoke of in the Youth Hostel. I could feel it so much I was there with you, naked, our skin red and stinging and the steam so fine licking the chill from our bones. Three years I haven't had a real bath or shower. We get to wash with hot water once every 10 days and only by scooping it out of a sink with a small hand-pitcher. A needle shower and a deep tub of bubble-bath and you to wash my weary body—a camel dreaming of an ice-cream cone…

I remember part of a poem I sent in the missing letter—something I liked:

Barbara bicycle somewhere in Europe,
pump the strong steady measure of your legs,
heartbreathing the land, a rolling world
beneath rolling wheels…
I would be a red streamer tassel swirling
and dancing your wind…
I would be a baseball card clothespin to the spokes—a low humming
in your mind as you moved through the morning…
I would be your hard leather seat…

And of course I keep your letters. They're in a box with Norman's.

Anyway, there's something coming. I can hear it in the air when I wake before dawn. And if you get down again remember that I'm holding onto you, Barbara, been doing it for a long time now, longer than you know…

Strength and love, Billy

11-23-73, Friday

Dad,

Good. I'll start at the beginning. This communication gap causes so much misunderstanding.

"If AF comes and I'm still here" refers, of course, to the possibility of some move by the U.S. Govt. which would 1.FREE ME or 2.TRANSFER me back to the U.S. It most certainly didn't refer to the interpretation which so upset you.

"...better than put our trust in the hands of lawyers..." is, I believe, self-evident. Questions:

—With the great amount of money paid them, what actually did Uge and Co. finally accomplish? I'm not saying what did they try and do, but what was their final resulting effort? 30 years. Didn't they conceal or even subtly lie to us about much that was happening behind the scenes? Why didn't they know about what was happening with my 4 year sentence? And if they knew, why weren't we informed?

Shoddy you met. He speaks in several directions at the same time.

All the lawyers want money before they act. I don't want any more money out to people before they produce.

My own failure was due not so much to planning as to lack of drive. There seemed to be no reason back then for not taking the leap when the opportunity presented itself. Today those reasons are insufficient to warrant caution in the light of my sentence. This does not mean foolishness is the word, rather that restraints are gone when the moment for action appears.

Equipment has been gradually obtained. But there is nothing in the wind to upset any of the possibilities outlined in your letter. We must wait for AF. AF must wait for government formation. The main purpose of my letter was to prepare you for the possibility that all these people—Buckley, Javits, Greene *[Senators Buckley and Javits, and Bob Greene at Newsday]*, etc, fail to accomplish our purpose. I pray for a solution along these lines but I am not so foolish as to place any great hopes in them. I believe only in you, in myself. I do not think it foolish or stupid to believe that God helps those who help themselves. My money is finished. I've hesitated writing because I <u>am</u> waiting to see what happens here with all this coalition-amnesty confusion. I wrote to Rob explaining a rather simple way of obtaining some quick cash. It is not all that difficult or dangerous, regardless of what you think from your perspective in N.Y. This sort of thing I watch happening all the time here.

I'll stop to get this in the mail tonight. Sorry to upset you but relax now—I'm holding on. Kind of quiet and tense like a coiled spring that waits its moment.

Love to Mom and all

Billy

P.S. Consul was just here with a fantastic full turkey dinner for us. It blew my mind. If you write them, know that these guys are really taking care of us.

11-28-73, Wednesday

My Dear Tibia,

Strange to hear you speak about my father. It seems that he and I have also had a bit of what might be termed conflicting viewpoints. But regardless, I wholly agree with you in saying it's one fine job he's doing—he is truly a fine father and friend. I know the reason for our disagreement and I've already written a letter which should bring the situation back into perspective. I think that the communication gap created by postal correspondence will become an ever more irritating factor as the time of promises and Amnesty passes and the time for serious endeavor begins. Our slight misunderstanding was over the proper time when one view of the picture should be shifted into the next. Kind of like making a film with two directors—but I reassured him that I'm still just sitting here playing the lead character in this weird shadowshow. Not to imply that I don't have a script of my own prepared should the Washington-Publicity Co. Inc. fail to bring their production to fulfillment. And then if it comes to my own number, well, I think you would appreciate the aesthetics of the idea. I mean, if the memory of the reason why we used to run the rhino-pits has not faded from your free-floating mind, then you can see the focus from behind which I'll direct my film...

But let us hope it is time for a break in the game and a full house Amnesty would be most welcome and appreciated...

I haven't the slightest clue as to the whereabouts of the SweetMan [a college buddy who went to Alaska the day after graduation, and never returned] but I did read something about a forest ranger in upper Alberta who reports seeing a strange unkempt animal vaguely resembling a naked Howler Monkey flitting through the trees and savagely dropping down upon all females large and small; and the ranger even purports to have seen this frightful creature attach itself to the hind quarters of a moose-calf then ride the poor bellowing animal across fields and streams and into the lake itself. It can't be Juan, because I think he's in Borneo, and it can't be Creamer, because he's in Mary in N.Y., and it can't be the Oat cause

he's doesn't like moose, being strictly a sheep man. So you take it for
what it's worth.

Keep the fires burning. I'll be along…

Love and regards to both you and the good Doctor

Finneus T. Bluster

12-30-73

Barb,

Been a lot of activity and apparent organization but as of this writing the Turkish government has failed to select a President or agree upon any form of coalition platform. Parliament is recessed now until Jan. 8th, when they are supposed to return to speak on the proposed Amnesty plan. The initial proposition for a 15 year general amnesty would leave me with almost 7 more years. The US govt. has been speaking with my father about some sort of action but I wonder just how much is talk and how much is actual fact. On December 28th, 3 Americans aged 28, 29, 30—two chicks and a guy, were sentenced to life imprisonment in a little Turkish town just this side of the Syrian border. They were busted almost one year ago with two carloads of dope, something like 100 kilos. They were actually sentenced to death but the court transmitted the sentence to life. I was a bit luckier—my life sentence was transmitted to 30 years. Hard to speak about activities on this level of existence without being thrown out of perspective by the sheer ludicrousness of it all. What I mean is that if the US is working in fact to release me, why weren't they able to help these other people? Perhaps the answer must wait for the forthcoming Amnesty. If the correct pressure is brought to bear and if God is in a particularly kind mood, perhaps there will be an article in the Amnesty dealing with the expulsion of all foreign prisoners. And my soul certainly does feel foreign to this place, even though I accept it as home, as where I am at this moment in time.

I believe it to be time for God to help those who help themselves but I am ready to wait until all other possibilities run their course.

If perchance I do happen to be out loose again in the near future, where will you be? Are plans arranged for winter? Will you stay at this hotel address? How long? Doing what? Why??

I think about a small place down by the ocean in southern Morocco—just naked sunshine of blue sky and so soft easy days of being absorbed back into that other way of existing. I would lie on my back in the sand, gazing the black depths of the velvet star night. I would wake mornings before dawn and pray my prayer of life— yoga to the earth and the ocean. And I would learn the softness of a woman's hand again. I would open again my soul and relearn the language of my body. I would reach within you and find myself...

Billy

1974

1-17-74, Thursday

Barb,

I tell you true that cold is just a word until you spend a few winters in here. The floors are stone, the walls and ceiling concrete. It's 6:20 am now and I've just come back up to my bed from the downstairs room. Yoga these mornings is really a test of strength for my new-found power of will. I mean at quarter to five when my head-clock goes off there isn't a soul stirring in here. Everyone's wrapped beneath all their blankets, full-clothed with sweaters and hats woolen pulled down over their ears. Fetal position is an absolute necessity. If you allow your extremities to stray too far out from the central heat of your groin, they numb up in a matter of minutes. 4:45 I stick my head out from my woolen cocoon and no shit my breath fogs the air. The windows have a thin layer of ice on this side of them—frozen fart condensation and foul stale stench of unwashed bodies.

It's been snowing light flurries for a week now and the overcast hasn't lifted since Dec. 30th. First thing I think of when I wake is how nice it would be to go back to snuggly sleep with my hand holding my stiff cock poking up through my longjohns. My body is insistent that its perception of the situation is totally correct and that there isn't the slightest doubt about the correct course of action. I mean, I'm full and swollen throbbing in my hand and the covers are warm and the air is cold and I haven't come in about a week and a half since my last wet dream because I've got this experiment going with masturbation abstention and God, but wouldn't it feel so fine to have you deep in my arms wrapped around me your woman love while we lick each other's mind…

Yeah, yeah. But you're far away and this is where I happen to be. And I've learned to observe and judge the perceptions and demands of my body. Sometimes I even direct them with my other brains. I know that it's necessary to gain a control of sorts over my physical, emotional, and intellectual brains. It's the most difficult thing I've ever attempted. Also the most important because it's what awareness is all about. So I don't go spewing my life-force on the toilet floor or feed some hungry young mouth. I attempt to channel my energies. Slowly, daily, minute by moment, I get there. Of course, sometimes I just don't give a shit and do what I feel—like beating off in bed and sleeping late or being moody and doing nothing or just quick-punching the first idiot who hassles me when he shouldn't.

And this Amnesty situation is not something that is conducive to smooth vibes. Christ, they been bullshitting around about this thing for 3 fucking years now. I mean, shit or get off the pot. The way it looks now, though, a government is on the verge of emerging from the political chaos that is the Turkish equivalent of the Democratic Process. And the head of the majority party of the coalition govt. says his first order of business will be granting an Amnesty. He's proposed a 15 year general amnesty which would still leave me with 6 years 8 months but perhaps there's more to it than that so we'll wait and see. I fully intend to make Morocco before too many months pass.

How long will you be in Klosters [*she got a job as a cross-country ski instructor at this fancy resort in Switzerland*]? Your big postcard, the first one with the letter, was a welcome piece of news. I'm glad for your happiness and your feeling for life vibes me so strong. The mountains and the stillness of snow on the forest. The real feeling of working till exhausted and then laughing, ready to face whatever tomorrow may bring along. I can't say about gorgeous creatures out of Vogue, but we have some amazing creatures here. I'd like to bring twenty of the choicest misanthropes of the prison over to your social scene in the resort. The place would never recover. Ah, a warm brandy and a roaring fireplace, bearskin rugs and hot cocoa and mayhaps even a small joint or two to mellow the mind. And have you seen anything of this Kohoutek fellow? With the artificial horizons of the walls and this two week overcast, it appears doubtful whether I'll be getting a glimpse of the comet or not. I was looking forward to seeing it but no big problem. Maybe I'll catch it next time around *[due back in 75,000 years]*. Door opening—

Bread has just arrived, sixty-two of them in a big canvas sack for the sixty-two prisoners here in the foreigner block. That's one bread a man but if you don't get downstairs and cop one right away, DING DONG, it's gone, some guy's eaten the whole thing and cleaned up the crumbs already.

I guess I could go on writing and talking to you page after page but now my stomach is yelling for some attention and since I denied my loins I'd better oblige my belly. Everything with balance. Must be a joke to hear me speaking about moderation. But then, what isn't a joke. Smiling at the insane loveliness of existence…

Touching you,
Billy

Marc,

Saturday
Feb. 8th

Fastback junky music blowing through my little black radio, the sons of Saint Door gone wild on the hurdy air out over the edge —

Just sitting here on my bed about 10:00 this sat. morn legs folded up under me for comfort and heat, sort of a tucked-in lotus that I've adopted for hours, years, sitting on flat-plank beds . . . me and the cat both hide our feet beneath us when we sit, it's the only to mesh with the cold in winter . . .

We have our first snow today . . . So fine to wake an see the magic transformation snow works on the prison. Out the window, the yard and opposite block have frailness, a softening of harsh angles and a muting of grey stone; it's like New York when the snow falls, covering the city with a muted emotion, a reflection or remembrance of naked men among the mountains, still and the silence of an Ice Age . . .

— 2:00 P.M. — but of course it doesn't hold, I've come in from two hours of snowball fights and soch in the slush of the yard . . . We skate a court with Turk kids about 12-17 years old — just had a mad football match in the wet slush snow slipping and sliding and lots of laughter . . . .

Yeah! Yeah! I dig it, flashing back to SF mornings when we were 17 and in your little red Sunbeam, the top down and our scarves flying out beh us in the blue-skyed winter wind, our destination

2-8-74, Saturday

Marc,

Fastback funky music blowing through my little black radio, the sons of Sam & Dave gone wild on the heady air out over the edge. Just sitting here on my bed about 10 this Sat. morning, legs folded up under me for comfort and heat, sort of a tucked-in lotus that I've adapted for hours, years, of sitting on flat-plank beds… Me and the cat both hide our feet beneath us when we sit, it's the only way to mesh with the cold in winter…

We have our first snow today. So fine to wake and see the magic transformation snow works on the prison. Out the window, the yard and opposite block have frailness, a softening of the harsh angles and a muting of the grey stone; it's like New York when the snow falls, covering the city with a muted emotion, a reflection or remembrance of naked men among the mountains, stillness and the silence of an Ice Age…

—2:00 pm—but of course it doesn't hold. I've come in from two hours of snowball fights and soccer in the slush of the yard… We share a courtyard with Turk kids about 12-17 years old—just had a mad football match in the wet slush snow slipping and sliding and lots of laughter…

Yeah! Yah! O dig it, flashing back to Sat. mornings when we were 17 and in your little red Sunbeam, the top down and our scarves flying out behind us in the blue-skyed winter wind, our destination any place in the world after the liquor store… God how I loved the big shopping centers, those bastard bazaars so apropos of the culture we grew up in and were shaped by… I mean wailing and humming around thru the buzz of those social hives, screaming wasps among the fat fumble-bumblebees, experience-eating energy-zapping fun-freaking fools, drunked out on wine and life, ripping loose from conditioning, the induced motivations of our affluent little Long Island society… I mean, mooning cops and stealing fucking medieval maces and such out from beneath the noses of store managers; bolting Chinese restaurants en masse…bolting the same goddamn diner three nights in a row with Wayne who was <u>so</u> crazy he even let himself get killed *[in Vietnam]* in defense of the great American motivation ("educational systems designed to motivate human beings toward acceptance of cultural heritage"—*Three Roads to Awareness*)—Prison's for the unmotivated...

Sunday night

After rereading it seems I got a bit carried away yesterday... It's heady stuff, communication, I can feel your presence strong and it sent me off... I miss you Marc, no spark-gap companionship here now—holed-up in the cave in the back of my mind a lot...

Monday morning

Back again—much confusion in here and extended periods of concentration aren't easy to come by... Writing to you was interrupted last night by an outrageous scene between these two Arab pickpockets from Saudi Arabia and Egypt—both of them are about 25 and zonged-out of their minds—got into some sort of altercation over a skuzzy little queer of a French junkie and before it was over windows were smashed and faces broken, one guy had his finger near bit off when he poked it in the other guy's eye but found his mouth instead...3 or 4 of the idiots who tried to interrupt the fight also began duking with each other—really a wearying sort of craziness that goes on all the time around here...

What with the fight and peace negotiations afterwards and the general emotional buzz of the atmosphere, I never got back to you until late—and it's impossible to stay awake reading or writing in here at nights, just too fucking cold—I mean, as it is in the air outside, so it is in the air inside, because we ain't got no non zero worth of heating—just farts and body stink to filter the cold air in here...shit, I'd rather sleep out in the snow in the yard, at least it's clean air...

But all this again is but a wandering of my pen—I mean to speak with you more frequently but this writing communication is difficult—so much to say in the way of friends who've been thru things together and been thru things alone...

And oh my! But can't I extend myself out and behind the wheel of that yellow Ferrari *[Marc sold high-end foreign cars]*... Yes, yes, the art form of the 20th century—sucked from the earth by the reaching hand of man, shaped from the curving airs of his mind... Motion, metamorphosis, metal madness, metaphors... Great sleek cock of a car hurtling off the ends of the earth...pull back on the wheel and aim just north of Arctaurus... Flame like a dying star and fuck the traffic lights...

Sheeeeeeeit! but I got to get out of this stale box of Rice Krispies... Soon, brother, got to reconnect with the earth. Get this steel-stone reverberance off of me... Big news in the way of 12 year Amnesty reducing me to 3 and 8 months—transfer request going in this coming week—result—good or bad—will be good as I'll know where I stand with that isle *[a request to be transferred to Imrali Island Prison in the Sea of Marmara]*...from that point of view it's good to go and good if they turn down the request because then I expect snow panes *[referring to the LSD escape plan]* to be so thick the fucking rhinos won't know me from a tick-bird and NYC here I come...

I'll write as there's specific news or sooner—

—Stay with that request, it's important.

—I'll let you know situation as it develops but keep in touch with me before coming or any such action—if it's necessary, I'll let you know...

And your gift for phrases is still superb—"There is no better prep for the real world than Indian Poker"—Oh yes!

Communication, yeah!

Love,

Billy

2-25-74

Barb,

A chill gray dawn, rainy Monday morning. The walls are gray, the bars are gray, the lockers are gray, the sky is gray, the air is gray…morning without meaning comes slow and choking for so many men here. It's a mental swamp, prison, oppressive, stagnating, shadowed with pitiful emotion-vultures and mind-vampires who must feed to live but do not dare drop upon a still-living heart-breathing man.

It's difficult to hold a balance here. Physical and mental self-preservation must be held in constant focus—a loss of perspective is especially dangerous—while at the same time I must strive to accomplish my purpose for being, which is simply, to love….I seemed to have discovered what might be called my 'thing'. At least I've discovered the only thing I can do, and do well, which has real meaning. I'm a transformer. I've learned how to attract the great energy vibrational love that flows all around our human ignorance and I've learned to send it flowing through and out of me. It's a gas. I can fill myself up and then send it all out in just a smile. I can feel it come flowing back strengthened and charged through the eyes of a friend, or a stranger.

It's nice to find what you're supposed to do. It's good to do it. It makes the air not so gray, it flavours and gives meaning to the sorrow. It makes me happy, Barb, it gives me peace.

You make me happy. A wind blows through your letters and it tastes so clean and free like it just came down off the mountains. Hold your friend and love him full and do not be afraid. Expect nothing and give everything and live with all your might. Ah, correction. Expect some news in a month or two. You'll either hear a first-hand account or read about it in the papers. Should be just like running the rhino pits at the zoo, or the bulls in the streets of Pamplona.

How long will you be there? Where next? Keep me posted on address changes. It will be easier to find you if I know where you are. And find you I will…

Love you

Billy

TUESDAY NIGHT
MARCH 12th 74

BONE,

So here I am again, standing on the ledge and wondering just how fast that fuckin ole rhino up the other end of the pit can run. MAN, you'll just have to excuse me not writing so often, but it's become difficult to write with my mind concentrating now only on dancing — the old two-step which the old man says he spoke to you about. The Consul has arranged for me to be transferred to a jail way the fuck over in the mountains of EASTERN Turkey. It's a weird place in the wilds where only the big-time sentence cons are sent — all killers and smugglers. Me an my two keys and 30 years gets me into the heavy-timer club. I'm supposed to give the word this week and they'll move the wheels in Ankara. I'm hesitant to say GO! only because there appears to be some new hope that our man in Ankara will be able to get me out with some kind of special amnesty. I just don't know what to think his chances of accomplishing this are but maybe I'll give it a few weeks. If he can't do something by then, well I guess I'll just

3-12-74, Tuesday night

Bone,

So here I am again, standing on the ledge, wondering just how fast that fuckin ole rhino up the other end of the pit can run. Man, you'll just have to excuse me for not writing so often but its become difficult to write with my mind concentrating now only on dancing—the old-two step which the old man says he spoke to you about. The Consul has arranged for me to be transferred to a jail way the fuck over in the mountains of eastern Turkey *[Kars Prison, near the Iran border]*. It's a weird place in the wilds where only the big-time sentence cons are sent—all killers and smugglers. Me and my two keys and 30 years gets me into the heavy-timer club. I'm supposed to give the word this week and they'll move the wheels in Ankara. I'm hesitant to say Go! only because there appears to be some new hope that our man in Ankara will be able to get me out with some kind of special amnesty. I just don't know what to think his chances of accomplishing this are, but maybe I'll give it a few weeks. If he can't do something by then, well I guess I'll just give word for the transfer to be worked and you'll remember how nimble the blond young man hopskippedandjumped across the Milwaukee Zoo...

Ah! the wines of Spain. Isn't it true that the wines of a land reflect and interpret the moods, the spirits, the very blood of its people? And where more than Spain is the great sorrowful joy of existence more intensely felt and sensed and breathed in the very air?

And if I should die on the streets of Pamplona and my blood chill the warm Spanish sun, let the wine on my lips tell the world that I lived loving life with all of my might...

The scene here will be static for a few weeks more, in which time I hope to hear some definite word from the Ambassador, and perhaps the Parliament will finish bullshitting about the AF. If you can, call Gills and Sabot and Arch and the others, T.J., to apologize for my long silence. I owe them all letters, not to mention so very much more. I'm sending a letter off to the Doctor when I mail this one.

He knows I'm a shiftless bastard so I'll surprise him with a letter. My greets to your folks. Keep your ears open for the sound of thundering hooves and keep your fingers clean…

    Crazy

3-13-74
Wed. morning
7:46a.m.

Marc, Melissa,

Listen, will it do just to say that I love you people and then I can eliminate the excuses for not writing in so many months? Been difficult to put words down onto paper. The muscles of my mind are tensing for a spring and this state is not conducive toward symbolic communication. There is a great buzzing confusion of vibrations within the walls of this prison. The sheer bumbling assininity of the government in all matters requiring the use of logic but in special regards to the long-proposed, much-expected, ever-coming, never-arriving General Amnesty proposal, is simply staggering in its magnitude. One morning the Minster of Justice will come shouting over the radio that he will have all the prisoners home in 'a warm nest' before the week is finished. That night the government makes a statement saying the Minister was misinformed due to his hereditary mental deficiency. Five different newspapers arrive the next morning with five different versions of just what progress, if any, Parliament is making on the AF. It is 5 months now since the Oct. 29th date which marked 50 years of glorious republic for Turkey. And every fucking day the AF rumors fill the air even more thickly than the great sweaty stink of 3000 unwashed men.

We had a hunger strike here a week ago. Seems like Hash offenders were being omitted from the AF so the jail flipped out and no one ate for a few days. The Minister of J. came and personally spoke to the excited animals and promised that he'd go speak to the AF commission and we'd all be included in the amnesty. You should have seen this cat—he looked like W.C. Fields in drag. I personally have turned off the deductive reasoning machine in my head and feed it no new info. I'll just wait to see what, if anything eventually comes of all this organized insanity. Mayhaps it's just strange enough that I go free but I doubt it so it looks like the two-step shuffle. (Bone's letter has more on this.)

Been keeping in touch with my soul and it seems to be moderately healthy if a little in need of soft rain and quiet sunshine and the light that shines in the eyes of friends. I haven't the slightest idea of what I'll do on the outside but I have a fair notion of who I'll be.

So drink deep and suck up the air, Springtime is coming. I wonder where Norman is, off somewhere kissing the erogenous zones of God...B

3-24-74, Sunday

Barbara,

I have a personal little philosophy of existence which places something called 'The Joke' at the base of all human activity. An understanding of The Joke concept cannot be accomplished by merely trying to grasp it with the intellect; it is far too enormously ephemeral to be encompassed by this most presumptuous of man's brains. It is necessary to <u>feel</u> the presence of The Joke; there is an element of absurdity involved here which cannot be fully appreciated by the intellect alone: the emotional center must contribute its own particular perspective. The Joke must be experienced. It's the reason I often find myself laughing for no reason at all.

Now, keeping all of this in mind, let me give you a quick chronology of one level of my life, i.e. the social criminal, for the past 4 years:

October 7, 1970—Busted Istanbul with 2 kilos of dope

Nov 1971—Sentenced in Istanbul (4 years 2 months)

Apr 1972—Sentenced rejected in Ankara

May 1972—Sentenced Istanbul (4 years 2 months); release date 7-17-1973

May 1973—(54 days before release) Sentence again rejected in Ankara—new court

Sept. 10, 1973—Sentenced to life, reduced to 30 years in Istanbul

March 12, 1974—Word received from Ankara, new review of case recommends new court, signs indicate good results, perhaps reduction to ten years, which would allow for my release when the Amnesty finally comes this Spring.

March 22, 1974—Court—lawyers absent, translator absent, Consul absent, adjourned until May 20, 1974.

March 23, 1974—I drop 3 tabs of Lucy's Sky Diamonds and sit on my bunk for 6 hours in perfect lotus bliss. At about 3 am I return to this ridiculous reality and begin laughing so hard I wake the whole block. When people ask me what's so funny, what am I laughing at, all I can say is "The Joke…"

So now I sit here and wonder just what is planned for the next episode. I've just completed all preparations for that shuffle-step production I wrote about in my last letters. But it seems as if it may not be necessary now. I don't know. Feels like I wandered onto the set of "The Marx Bros. in Istanbul" movie and Fellini is directing. Anyway I'll write on Friday after Consul visit.

Love, Billy

3-28-74, Friday

Barbara,

Where are you? Are you all right? I'm feeling the absence since your last letter and there is something troubling in the air... I'm concerned about your leg: last letter you were writing from propped-up legbound position and I thought what it would be like to be there and cook your food for you and talk with you for hours and laugh and touch and fill up on each other with maybe me going out for walks in the morning and the evening to just <u>see</u> things and stretch myself out a bit and would I feel soooo fine to be coming back to you with your smile waiting in your eyes and maybe people on your street would know me in a few days as the newest but probably the oldest of your lovers and wouldn't <u>that</u> make me feel so fucking good I'd be going around all the time like some laughing fool...just be together for a while until leg is O.K. and then flow as we will...will be...I am not able to extend out towards the future with any details of time and place—so difficult some of the quirky angles of this rulered reality about me here—it disjoints my mind to not be able to say to you "Stay put! exactly where you are while reading this letter because I'm following after it. I arrive..." When? Tomorrow? Yeah, and when is that? I just don't know. It rips me up.

Write me, Barb, I want to know about it all. I have petty news that can wait until next letter.

Keep believing,

Love,

Billy

4-23-74
Tuesday morning
12:07 am

Barbara,

Your letter and the stillness of the night and so many things so wrong and so many things so right. I feel like I'm dying here at times. The dead coldness of the stone quickly sucks up what little warmth, what little love people manage to create between themselves, within themselves. It's difficult for me to stay aware, to send out the vibrations I should if I am to be true to my reason for being. In here I've learned that my strength is not my mind but my emotions. I've also learned that it is this same emotional power that has led me in its untamed wake and helped whirl the days of my sweet life in such a windblown pattern. Most definitely not to attempt to subdue but definitely to somehow guide and direct my strength— this is the work that is meaningful for me. It's so hard here without any help, to be a companion along this strange road toward God. My friend, Nick, went free last week. Just some 20 year old English freak who got busted 2 years ago with a little dope in his pocket. Just a tall slow spooky kind of Catholic lunatic who patiently, ploddingly brought me to realize how little I knew about most everything; and stranger still, how much I unknowingly knew about other things, important things like laughing and feeling people and loving life. I'm missing Nick but his presence remains, just as crazy Norman remains with me even with his body two years in the earth…

It's been hard these past months. So many plans and possibilities seem to have fallen apart. It's getting hard for me to breathe, the air is heavy and weighted with time. I smell the sea wind sometimes in my dreams. I walk the yard in the morning, cement earth beneath my feet and clouds of birds in my hair.

Spring is here and I'm trying not to be hasty but I so need some softness. My eyes would drink in fields of flowers. I would hear God in the silence of the mountains. Life would rest on my tongue such a sweet fruit—-and its taste would be Barbara…

Questions and answers: same place, new name. I have your letters, they charge me, give me strength. I feed on you, woman. My wall is mountain and sky *[a panoramic mountain-top view she sent me]*—fantastic, I gaze for hours.

News about Amnesty and getting out—tangled, complicated. I am patient only for those people, my parents and friends, who are trying so hard. I don't know how much longer I can wait. A Gordian knot, a sword in my hand, and strength in my arm...

Gordian knots, umbilical chords, lines of sanity, strings of words...

Don't let go, Barb, hold us...

Billy

5-1-74, Sunday

Hello Folks,

Just thought it was time for a little report from the eastern front. By now you've probably heard from Congressman Murphy and Bob the Chicago-Trib reporter, so I'll pass that news by. But some other unusual happenings. While I was thinking about my chess game *[code for escape plan, the hospital report being a first step]* I fell and hit my head last Monday evening. Seems to have been some sort of mild concussion, so Wed. morning I went off with two soldiers to make the round of the hospitals. Eventually, the doctors couldn't be sure of any damage but since I was in pain and vomiting they thought it best if I rest in the hospital a few days. I came back last nite feeling better though my eyes bother me a bit, can't quite focus right and gives me a slight head-ache. I'll go back to the doctor again to see if all is well and perhaps I'll need glasses or something. I don't know yet. I'm just resting easy now and playing chess.

Looks like Amnesty should be along soon—a couple of weeks maybe. Will be a strange time with so many people going free from here. I'll still wait to see what, if anything, Mac *[Ambassador William Macomber]* is doing. I really doubt if he can accomplish much, but don't doubt at all that he's trying his best.

Tuesday I'll be off to court. Seems like my 19,000 T.L. fine will be dropped. Better to pay the fine and drop the 30 year sentence, but so it goes.

Spring has arrived here. Warm and beautiful. I hope all of you are well there. I know the strain this all is on you.

Dad, you asked about my friend Ben *[Franklin—$100 bills]*. He's doing well. I've needed his help a few times with some 'chess problems' and his advice is good. We're both waiting patiently for the AF to see what may be forming with Uncle Mac.

Its' too bad about your moustache but Mom will be happy to know that mine is coming on strong again. Looks like some crazy yellow caterpillar has taken up residence just below my nose.

Question of sorts? What's the story on that Defense Fund? Ben and I are interested of course. The more the merrier. If someone's holding the strings it's time to tell them to let go.

So I'll write definitely next week after the court and Consul visit. Love to all of you and keep smiling...

Billy

5-5-74, Friday

Marc,

Obviously been my fault for our much dwindled correspondence but in truth you must admit you haven't exactly been a fucking Guttenburg Galaxy yourself. I had to go to court again today for some ridiculous piece of Turkish irony. Seems the court reviewers in Ankara feel my sentence of 30 years is adequate and it would be cruel and excessive punishment to further burden my karmic wagon with a money fine so today we go through the formalities of removing $1,357 dollars and 14 cents from my Debit-to-Society column. Which leaves me with a mere 16 years, 5 months. Of course, Amnesty is now just a hair away, needing only the President's signature, and this boon by the grace of Allah would reduce my time to 11 years 5 months, which is such exciting news it almost gives me an erection.

But I've been hearing some encouraging news from the front and concerned officials appear to be gathering their political paraphernalia—the possibilities are such that foolish speculation is uncalled-for in view of the ridiculous reality.

I myself have been running my hot hands up under the robes of Lady Justice (who is actually little Miss Luck) and the response is edifying if not enthusiastic. The Consul people say just a few more months and we'll know what they can or can't accomplish. I'm doubtful but hopeful and will grant the people who are working these lines at least a few more months patience. But it's moving on, my life, and a gear change is necessary if the motor is not to burn itself out. I have a friend of mine named Joey who'll be going out with the Amnesty and then flying to New York. I've given him Bone's address and he'll be getting in touch. I think you dudes will all get on fine since he's as crazy as I remember you two being 4 years ago, and I certainly can't imagine either of you have changed in that respect. Perhaps a night of wine and smoke and you'll hear from him just what the situation is here. I don't know when he'll arrive but it should be sometime in the coming weeks *[Joey never did arrive]*.

I'm writing all the above in the early raindropped morning and now at 8:37 they're calling my name on the loudspeaker box attached to the peeling-plaster wall...Villyam HA-Yes, Villiyam Hayes, *cok* quick get your unbeliever butt down to the exit block the court-car is waiting... Let the fucker wait... Just finishing a sweet coffee the texture of sand-silt, like the fin-fanned sand of a carp nest under muddy water. Drink a lot of coffee now. The tea is like weasel piss.

In a few minutes the guards will come banging on the door downstairs, yelling for me to come out, got to get to court. They'll be loud but no sweat, these guys know me now and they don't bite the hand etc... The head guardian in charge of the prison is another matter altogether and I flash to pleasant thoughts of tiny needles tipped with curare and remember what a good shot I used to be with a pea-shooter...

—In the basement of the courthouse, waiting to be taken upstairs. It's a square block gloomy room, 15 paces across, wet cement floor, two faded yellow bulbs hanging from the high ceiling on worn wires. A small toilet is blocked off in one corner—stinks the whole room up. Eight old wooden benches with pacing men back and forth thru the cigarette smoke floating gray in the yellow light. Windows up at ground level but barred and screened to hold us in and the light out.

When they finally get to taking me up to court they'll chain my hands together—linked iron around my wrists.

I've got a nice suit I won in a poker game but don't have it on now. Fuck it, dungarees and my leather jacket are good enough for this.

Thirty-nine people locked in the back of the court-wagon that carried us here from the prison. A bit crowded but I managed a place near the window so got some flashing views of Outside as we rolled through Istanbul. Ah, man, I tell you, I drink life thru my eyes. There were trees and flowers and one chick looked like a tourist who was so fine I'm sure she felt my eyes straining to suck her right in off the street... But then the car moved on and she was gone...

—Back from court. How I hate those fucking chains. The soldiers who went with me were nice dudes who smelt strongly of the heat and offered me their condolences on my 30 years.

Melissa, I must apologize for not returning your letter. It's just that I grow stale and stagnant here and find writing to people easier to do tomorrow. Perhaps by then there'll be more to say. But I know it's necessary to live today so I direct my energies toward keeping myself balanced. It seems like so long since I was close to the softness of a woman. The complementary vibrations of male-female. I miss the energy created in the merging.

—Haven't been writing much this past year. Too extended by the possibility-lines involved with the scene. I look forward to the relative calm that will descend on the prison when 2500 of the 3000 prisoners go free with the Amnesty. I've begun scheduled work [writing] again and hope to work steadily these next few months waiting for official plans to work themselves to their eventual conclusions. After that....well, Joey will be better able to explain the difficulties to you...

—If Spring has come to New York as it has to Istanbul I wonder if there are vibrations stirring there that can reach out across the distance to touch me here. I've been feeling some strange stirrings lately...but then I've always felt strange stirrings. It seems things have risen from the depths of my being that might never have arisen had it not been for the weight of prison. The more it presses down the more necessary it becomes to counter the weight with some inner stanchions. I think I'll have a direction into other dimensions should I ever leave this place. Just where this all will lead and end I haven't the slightest idea. But it's not so important where you're going as long as you know where you are. Life is really something I know nothing about but appreciate immensely in spite of my ignorance.

Love, strength, laughs
Willie
P.S. lost my address book, guessing

5-18-74, Sunday

Marc,

Well now look, friend, I find it hard to believe you couldn't find some way to fulfill my request but then this may be in part due to the distance at which I perceive the situation outside... O.K...so allowing that it's just vaguely possible that you couldn't find any way shape form to satisfy the request *[LSD for an escape plan]* I'm so urgently awaiting, I still can find no reason for not hearing from you in regards to this matter...

I mean, I wrote you Feb 25th and received a reply from you soon after saying you'd be in touch with some news shortly... Come on, Marc, this is 3 months later and although I've written you again March 30th, I still haven't heard any more from you... And then yesterday my brother writes saying he contacted you and that you'll be writing soon... Well fucking hell don't you realize what I'm doing with these requested little superfleas. I mean, you are aware of the Pilgrim State routine, *[refers to the huge mental hospital on Long Island, and my plan to escape from Bakirkoy]* waiting just out in the wings, but I tell you it just won't get on stage as long as I'm playing the lead because the play I've written myself will bring down the house with applause or bring out the fucking hook...I mean the huu-kay (Vonnegut)...

Very nice relating news in the form of a 7 year sentence reduction finally becoming official on May 12th, so as of this writing my release date is October 7th, 1978... And my transfer request was accepted April 10th by concerned officials in Ankara...with the resulting news being that soon after the official reduction is finished, a decision will be forthcoming... As you can well imagine I am anxiously and hopefully awaiting this decision... It has been too many years since I've seen green trees and felt earth beneath my feet... It would be so fine if I could work in fields on this island... So fine to be close to nature again after so long surrounded by stone... So I am expecting news about this momentarily, and all the while my request figures in weaving strings of this magic carpet agrowing... So now

I'm wondering if it's just a specific difficulty as regards windowpanes or is it just a general scarcity or a lack of contacts... I mean shape and form can and must be malleable... I mean if you gotta, you gotta, so there are many and varied modes of transport just as there are many and varied modes of communication... And in this most ungainly form we're using now I can't explain as I'd like to but I must say to you that it's really down to 'Do you wanna? Or not...??' (Actually I could use five hundred or a thou but think I can get by with the fifty requested)...

So write me here at this same address with news and letters but perhaps important letters or books etc should be mailed to me c/o The American Consulate, Tepabasi, Istanbul, and then if I'm already at another prison—*Inshallah [God willing]*—they'll forward it along...

And I must say it blows my mind to hear from Bone after 3 months silence and he tells me he's getting married...and I imagine the wedding would be a fine place to see a lot of old friends gathered together for a spot of merry madness...oh yes, oh yes,...the sweet mad whirling...

Billy

6-7-74, Thursday

Folks,

White kite on a blue sky, with a white chalk moon just rising over the yardwall on a summer afternoon. And here I sit. Up the opposite end in the shade. Got lots of sun this morning. Lots of martens, swallows, and a great stork high up above them, soaring the clouds. Great calm mountains of clouds.

The noon press interview with *Newsday's* reporter here was a gas. Far out to actually come in contact with someone involved with all this. I mean, all this publicity, be it helpful or harmful, is just a bit astounding for me. I've been suddenly shaken out of my quiet pleasant little scene and suddenly being vibed from all sides with this great rush of outside energy. I've tuned myself into quite a different frequency in here, so you'll have to excuse this delay in writing. The past week's news has only been assimilated today upon speaking with the journalist. I mean, it's really moving with momentum now, isn't it? I wonder if anyone really knows where all this will lead but hell it doesn't matter because off we go and it's always here and now. Isn't it...

So you say they want some writing from me. That may be difficult since my vocab and ideas seem ill-suited for the daily press. Excuse me, but my expressions and observed interpretations of prison life and Turkish Mental Hospitals and such just may be a bit harsh for the daily reader.

And I have come to believe that much of my early work was like pissing in a tin can because you like the sound of the tinkling. The last eight months have brought some strange perspectives to my eyes—when I turn them in or out they see colours of meaning beyond the old borders of my knowledge.

I'll send some fragments of observations *[enclosed The Wall, below]*—some old stuff, some notes, some ideas. Let me know if it interests anyone there. It will be a good exercise of discipline to see if I can express with these little squibs of symbols all the weirdness, the strange absurdity I find around me; if I can explain to you how it is possible for me to say I sit here in a calm place and none of this really touches me. How it just isn't as important as it used to be. I want to be free, to touch all you people again, to walk in the rain alone in the night, to smile into friends and love the light in their eye. But I could stay here if I had to. This is only a prison if you see it with prison eyes. It is a monastery early morning when I rise. It is home during the day. It is a community of people, some aware of it, all God...It is where I am...

So let's get it on with what we have. Will write Sunday.

Love

Billy

P.S. No fears. Health is good. Slight cough. Bushy moustache.

"The Wall"

The stonecold yardwall is all drab grey cement. It stretches up about 30 feet with a small overhang of lip. I don't mind it anymore. At first I used to hate the thing, stab it with my eyes and will it crumbled, blasted ruin. But now time brings understanding and the wall just borders the sky.

Sometimes, if I scatter breadcrumbs, it even provides a perch for pigeons who drop in for a feed. They silhouette up there—30, 40, 50 birds against the lightening morning sky. The wall doesn't mind them, just as it doesn't mind me. It just stands there being itself— kind of sad and lonely, unhappy but not at all ashamed. Separating things will do that. It just accepts its purpose. It isn't expected to like it. I mean, it isn't a tree or a waterfall or a cloud. Then it would be easy to be happy. And it isn't a man either—then, at least, it would be possible. It's just a wall and knows it.

So I don't think badly about it anymore. It just wouldn't be right. But sometimes, when I'm near to brimming with pain or frustration, I go out early when the door first opens and press my body hard up, face to this great grey wall—and I try to feel it totally with my palms and cheeks and loins. I would love this thing of cold loneliness if I could. But it does not know of love and it isn't deserving of hate.

It's just a wall.

So I softly scream of sorrow and listen for an echo. And the pigeons still sit quietly watching, waiting for me to move on; and the sky takes on the day; and the wall moves not one iota. But somewhere deep within, there is a response; a complementary chord struck—a vibration. And weight is drawn from me. I seem to rise up light and can get on with the important business of just living every day.

I think maybe the wall soaks up the pain. If you just accept it then it does what it can to help. It can't break apart to let me out—this isn't in its nature; it's a wall. But it can absorb sorrow. It will bounce back hatred and not know how to hold love—but it accepts the weight of sorrow. This is in its being. A wall is solid sorrow, it separates things. It will take the weight from those who understand...

Against the Wall, c. 1974—Which four are going free soon and which two aren't? l. to r., Pino, me (with zinc oxide nose), Jacques (seated), Patrice, Ding Dong, Harvey.

6-30-74

Barb,

So here it is, Sunday afternoon again. In the sunbaked heat of the yard I can see June sliding quietly into July. I'm at a table in the downstairs room because it's cool and empty down here. Just Patrice with his guitar. Practicing classical sounds against the echoed corner-walls. He goes out in December. Had a 12 year sentence reduced by AF. I've made a bet with him that I'll be out first. I plan to win, easy way or hard way.

But that's another level of reality. Been reading *The Passion of the Mind*, by Irving Stone. Quite good presentation of life and basic concepts of Sigmund Freud. After reading *The Agony and the Ecstasy* I'd been looking around for more books by Stone. Michelangelo simply staggered me with his intensity for living. At one point, in his early days of blindly groping step by step thru the dark unknowns of the human mind, Freud found himself in need of neurosis cases. He learned, taught himself the methods of psychoanalysis, building and learning with each new case. I was reading of this at about 3 am one morning and then burst out laughing thinking what a psychiatrist's paradise this place is. We have the strangest kind of scenes come bubbling up from those repressed oppressed sources. The weirdness about this place is that few of the people here know who's a doctor and who's a patient, including their own assortment of projected images. I keep flashing onto Big Chief Bromden in *One Flew Over the Cukoo's Nest*. Yeah, I'm invisible here sometimes, an alien character observing the machinations within some strange cosmic metaphor…

Lots I want to speak with you about but the wind is up and we're only waiting for the T's to give the O.K. and up anchor! Off we go. Stay in touch with yourself…

Love
Billy

7-24-74

Barb,

Sitting out in the yard after the rain has stopped, eating a fresh peach, and what a fucking treat it is, I must say. Our produce must come from the city and it's been quite disorganized, the delivery and sale, since the AF. It's only in the past week that things have gotten back together. I do fully appreciate nature's sweetness holding a piece of fruit in my hand.

Just went and got a lifeguard haircut because summer has really been sweltering here this year. I kind of was hoping to grow it a bit then let it fly on the Outside but looks now as if the wait may be longer than expected. And I can handle the heat and the sweat from yoga merits a cold washing afterwards but there isn't always water available so I got the barber to cut it all off. And went ahead and shaved it with a razor, done it up all the way, so must be careful not to get my scalp sunburned, shaving this late in the summer.

I'm actually pretty wound up about this whole patience scene. I mean there is now the Cyprus problem *[Turkish troops invaded Cyprus in July, 1974]* added to the Opium production question and here I sit waiting for an imperial nod, the old upraised thumb…timing seems to be off a bit. I feel marionette strings tangling in the air over my head… Ah, Pinocchio, slipping your lines and stealing off under the cloak of madness…

Just can't get much together in the way of words to you. The war has closed the airport for the past week and no letters have been collected until today. And I would speak with my eyes and the tips of my fingers, share some mornings with you then see where life leads. Don't know for sure about anything but appears if the 'operation' is a success, I'll be reborn Caesarian section and shunted to NY, which would mean passing over you at a height of 20,000 feet but I'll shout out the window and you'll hear me. I hope it can be a natural birth—Morocco lures me so, but I just don't know.

Waiting waiting waiting fuck waiting I want to breathe deep the air of the ocean, the wind in your hair…

Love
Billy

8-4-74, Sunday

Marc,

It would appear that the negotiations which we've all been waiting for are going to take longer than expected. I've been holding off from writing anyone because, as you said in your last letter, I wondered if I might arrive before my letter did. But this doesn't seem to be the case now, with the Cyprus situation usurping my action, so I guess it's time to pen some symbol sounds.

I sent you a 10 page letter on the 17th of May. Unfortunately I had to guess at the address and sent it off to G.T. Glen Cove. Bone informs me of my mistake so I have to assume you never received it. Too bad, was a lot of strange thought involved.

Summer's gripping the prison in its hot hands. The cement canyonyard absorbs and retains the heat so that you can't even sit on the ground, it's so hot. The prison is emptied out to a great degree now that Amnesty has come and gone. This helps a bit. Only 25 guys on my block now, where formerly were 75. This is still one too many, but nothing to do but wait now that I'm playing along with the official-action troupe. I don't want to seem ungrateful but it certainly is taking a long time for these people to get their act on stage. Indications are that I'll be shuffling along home soon, so I guess I can wait a while longer for them to get it together.

Bone wrote asking for some suggestions as to what the two of you could do in the way of alternate planning, in case this program is scratched before it opens on Broadway. Actually, there isn't anything needed at this point. If the politicos can't come across with their script, I have all that is necessary for a one-man band, complete with Tuba, suzaphone, and electric glockenspiel.

It is truly a staggering conception to imagine that I might actually be in the ocean again soon. My dreams are coloured with the soft sighing sounds of seawind, and women weave in and out of the waves.

I don't really know what it will be like to be free again. I've been able to encompass the fact of 4 years Inside only by observing numbers on a calendar and abstract news from the media. I know that the changes in the outer world will be exaggerated to a mind-boggling degree for someone who's seen only gray-stone walls for so long. Friends who have left here have written back, speaking of the traumatic readjustment that takes place. Personally, I doubt if I'll ever re-adjust to life as I once knew it. This is a positive aspect of prison, not a negative. So much taken for granted before. So many small wonders taken as given. There's no way I can begin to plan anything other than just living each day as if it were the first and last day of existence.

So you've been breathing through a straw, huh *[Marc broke his nose in a car accident]*? Well, at least you're still breathing. I doubt whether the pace of New York City will be to my liking after so long in this wax museum. I've ideas about travel and such but practical factors weigh heavy in any moves I make. I owe many people so much, money not the least of my debts.

It's been a strange morning for concentration. A whole herd of guards have been across in the kid's block which is opposite ours on the other side of the courtyard. 12-18, a true pack of young animals they are. Seems that late last night one of the new kids got gang-raped and this morning there's been one hell of a commotion over there. Just the normal sort of happening for a Sunday morning. Environment and its effect on human beings. Christ! What a looney bin this place is.

Barbara was here for a visit a few months ago. Really good to see her and feel the warmth and happiness she exudes. Been traveling, mountain climbing, flowerbreathing and life loving. She and I find complementary vibrations in our letters. She's back in Switzerland now. Summer and blue sky and the sound of clear mountain streams.

And for Melissa—what can I say to excuse my lack of writing. Only that I'm dry now. I don't do much in the way of words. No stimulus, stifled vibes and dead stone. I'm containing now. Just trying to hold steady against the pull. Don't want to shrivel up inside like so many people around me. I need a watering very bad. Life-rain and sea-soul and the softness of quiet mornings with people I love.

I'm not so sure of some things I used to know and I know about some things I was never very sure of...life and Karma and the Cosmic Joke...Tickled at the thought of God laughing thru his long white beard...

Love,
Billy

8-18-74, Sunday

Folks,

I'm upstairs in the library writing you a letter. Yes, there's a library here in the prison. Four years I'm here and I've never known it existed until just recently when it was re-opened. It had been closed since the riot 4 years ago and now a prison psychologist has been sent out from Ankara after the Amnesty and has decided to re-open the library. Quite a nice guy he is. Not a guard or a prisoner but a civilian doctor. He's working hard to alleviate the many problems existing here. I was lucky to have met him early and now helping to arrange and index the great dusty piles of books that have accumulated over the years. Seems like the periodic controls here have taken a great number of English books—I'm finding books that were taken away 4 years ago.

It's cool and quiet here. Quite a change from the cellblock. I'm just biding my time, listening to the news out of Ankara and following the Cyprus situation with great interest. You should have spoken with Gene Zajac by now and I know Mike Griffith has talked with you. Was really good for me to see him and hear some first hand news. I hope some kind of word comes down in the coming days. It's difficult to watch another summer drift past. My body craves the ocean and I'm anxious to see all of you again now that it seems so close.

You'll have to excuse me for not writing but I keep thinking perhaps I'll arrive before my letter. If this is wishful thinking on my part that's <u>exactly</u> what it is. I feel that this may actually be the end now and 4 years worth of waiting has dried up my pen.

Anyway, I'm feeling quite good and healthy and hopeful. Let's just see what goes on now that Cyprus is finishing. Not another delay, I hope.

I'll try to get a decent letter together soon. Maybe deliver it by hand.

Love to all,
Billy

'94 Thursday
August 22d

Barb

Hmmm, ummm, well... yes. I believe the rain
Arcing earth to air to earth, so timely revealed for
your eyes... multi-hued symbol structure, silent
sign in the sky... colours of life and the
obscuring white reality of shrouding fog wrapping you
in your veiling individuality, your loneliness), your
ever-stretching instant of awareness.... A long way
back to the source. I don't think many make it, I
think the loneliness stops most. It's hard to focus through
tears. It's hard to hear the sweet hum of life sometimes
when emptiness seems to stretch from without to within
and you just don't know whether you're sucking it up or
breathing it out..... The summer of my 19th year
Marc and I were winding down some mountain road
approaching Geneva. Our old Spanish bike was so happy
to be finished the long pull up that it leapt with
sheer joy down the slope. Marc drove with his
usual efficient abandon, singing Wooly Bully over and
over while I hung on the back with our knapsack
drinking spanish wine) and wind and sucking up life
with all my senses. We turned a bend in the road
and there below us down in the valley was a great
sky-cloud rainbow come to earth. It just hung
an arch of light across the road. I mean it
was staggering both ends touching the wet
green of bordering fields and this intense bridge

8-22-74, Thursday

Barb,

Hmmm, ummm, well…yes…I believe the rainbow arcing earth to air to earth, so timely revealed for your eyes *[from her recent letter]*…multi-hued symbol structure, silent sign in the sky…colours of life and the obscuring white reality of shrouding fog wrapping you in your veiling individuality, your loneliness, your ever-stretching moment of awareness… A long way back to the source. I don't think many make it. I think the loneliness stops most. It's hard to focus through tears. It's hard to hear the sweet hum of life sometimes when emptiness seems to stretch from without to within and you just don't know whether you're sucking it up or breathing it out… The summer of my 19th year Marc and I were winding down some mountain road approaching Geneva. Our old Spanish bike was so happy to be finished the long pull up that it leapt with sheer joy down the slope. Marc drove with his usual efficient abandon, singing "Wooly Bully" over and over while I hung on the back with our knapsack, drinking Spanish wine and wind and sucking up life with all my senses. We turned a bend in the road and there below us down in the valley was a great sky-cloud rainbow come to earth. It just hung, an arc of light across the road. I mean, it was staggering— both ends touching the wet green of bordering fields and this intense bridge of colour against the black rain sky. I said Ah yes, now if that isn't a portent I just don't know my magic. And it was, too. I mean, Life has been truly good to me and for me. Never can tell about the years in here either. Time is perspective needed to assess the meanings of all this.

I got a good feeling about you, seeing you there on the mountain with that rainbow in your eyes. Rainbows don't last forever. Ours folded before we could pass under it. Yours dissolved into mist which rose up to wrap around you. Fine event, woman, should make up for a lot of misbalance caused by the world of ignorance and pain…and people…

And now the goat in the triangle of calves *[another reference from her last letter].* Yes, what now if that goat was actually a ram, oh I could tell you about Aries *[my sign]* and triangle symbology and the fertility of the grass but I'm not going to because I'm thinking about you. I'm reading your words and I'm hurting that some of the flavors of life have become stale for you. Barbara Barbara to roll naked in the long green grass of a mountain meadow and lick the sweet wet dew from your body…

I don't know what to say about Nancy *[her sister brought her much love and pain]* and friends other than environment, influence, and remember yourself before the road and the awakening of consciousness… I guess it will be something of a cultural shock to whisk out on a plane and 14 hours later be in New York again. I actually don't want to do it like that at all… But then alternatives are few and not too inviting. I had planned a small hotel room and a shower and a slow stroll through a world of sensory impressions, tastes, sight, light, walking a straight line in one direction for hours, breathing the sea… Slowly moving toward Switzerland and you…then moving down to southern Morocco for a while… maybe arriving in N.Y. in 3 months or so. This way (if I ever get gone) is a plunge in arctic water after a sauna.

It's weird. Had N.Y. lawyer-friend *[Mike Griffith]* here visiting a month or so back. Young competent good-looking dude who blew my mind just relating some of the social scene changes. Turns out he and I have several mutual friends. He gave me good news but was honest enough to say that although he and all concerned were extremely confident, he did say that time was an unknown factor. Since we're waiting for the T's. And then he left for a 3 week vacation on Mykonos. And immediately Cyprus blew up.

He's back in N.Y. now. If and when I go via the Transfer Train, he'll be back to fly back with us (me and Fed fuzz). He's talking about a book and things like tube interviews and the whole show. I will admit that it tantalizes me while at the same time scares the living shit out of me thinking about all those mixed emotion vibes coming down. But if some bread can be obtained from this direction

I'm all for it. I don't even want to tell you what kind of money debts I've piled up these past 4 years.

Summer sliding over me. Drawing pictures of Morocco and pencil sketches of clowns in alleyways. August 8th Nixon resigned. Seems to be a happening day, no? 8888888888....I don't know, just babbling away when there's so much I want to talk with you about. Later. Time and significance and soft words wrapping real meaning...

Smiling, you know why...

Billy

Friday, August 30th, 1974

Words to Barbara

Full moon in a still sky and a jet a brightly beaded moth
roaring across my night...quiet prison of echoes
and far off sounds...
metal vibrations in the stone wall against my head
—step treads of heavy feet, tired rounds,
hollow pipe rumblings...
at the window and far beyond the mournful calling
of some lonesome ship out in the harboring darkness...

Words strung out, drifting in motion...
patient...potential...
a scattering, a net,
a sack of symbol sounds strewn forth then
drawn tight with the implosive power of a prick
thrust up into hungry loins...

Words and the spirit flowing thru them,
hallowed mist around the moon
and a fart from the bed above...

From meditation a balance
that can never be held lest it be lost...perspective...
poetry...

And from this somewhere-point of existence a pulse
surges out in all directions,
across all the universes, pulsing
individual being into That Which Is...and sucking
that which is down into my pen...

Four years at the window
and I'm still looking thru the bars...

but I'm also looking at them…very close I am…
and well now lookee here don't they appear
like they ain't so strong after all
and like I couldn't just snap one…easy…
by just closing my fucking hand…
hmmm…ummmmm…now no need to get angry…
taken the good part of waiting, which is
not worrying, and now got to hold still
for the bad part of waiting, which is
waiting, waiting…natch…

Yeah, clouds are breaking up
and the moon's come out just above the horizon
of the far wall…rain still sounding, echoes
in the thin tin dripplings off the spouts…
but stars are coming out again
and the storm is almost over, moving off now
somewhere down the coast…

Roosters out there somewhere ruffling their feathers
and shaking out their voices…so settling somehow
to hear them drifting in to me
past the bars and grunts and snores…
I feel the earth beneath their scrabbly feet,
know the dawn in their raggedy song…

Goddamn but it feels good to crow at the night
when you know the sun's coming up strong behind you…
and don't I cut the silhouette now, don't I…?...

Ah, Barbara, the nights we spend awake
alone…together…writing so we don't scream
or cry…writing to send something
or to seal something or just because we want to…
writing because we must…

And I guess that with words being like thought
and thought being Life, then I'm sending you
a little piece of my life here, a little piece
of the god that I am...
have a hunk of God, there's lots
to go round...

There's goes another jet...You'd think they'd have a little consideration plotting their take-off pattern over a prison...

Getting time to sleep, I think...Sure could do with a swim in the ocean before I nod out...Ah, Yes, the things we take for granted... look, look, here comes the sun...

Love, Billy

PART 2

Gotten around to Sunday afternoon now... A letter from Nancy finally arrived yesterday. All the Belmonts seem to have such good eyes for the life around them at the moment... It was her birthday, 24, and a fresh white-swan May day I felt rise from her letter...

She mentioned something about another *Newsday* article...You know, I find it truly amazing that so many people read about this weirdness I'm enmeshed in here... I think the publicity gig and media exposure when I arrive back in N.Y. is going to be just a pisser and a half—I mean, fucking televison interviews and these talk-show radio things... I've already been contacted by some T.V. outfits for doing a spot here at the prison, but we decided to reject this for diplomatic reasons (which pissed me off even though I saw the reasoning of it)... I mean it will be so strange after this semi-entombment here for so many years now... But I just couldn't face that weirdness until after at least a couple of months cooled out on the beach of Morocco or some similar simple nature scene, where a rhythm I'm attaining can be tuned to the pitch of the world. Oh my how sweet it is to be alive...tears and all, it's just a groove...whatever follows this life as a next step will be an even groovier position, assuming it's a next step... Yes yes I like the line—"...Just some crazy Christ on a bike, moving toward the smiling light…" *[from Barbara's bicycle trip around Europe]*.

Got your Eskimo book—fantastic, I'm sending another one off to you that I was fortunate in obtaining just at the same time (timing, yes, yes)… It's great… I'm ½ way thru *The Idiot* but picked up some Faulkner books and he always takes precedence in my readings…

Love you Barbara,
Billy

10-18-74, Friday

Folks,

Yes, I know it's been a long time since I wrote last but strange events been going on and I've been awaiting their conclusion before trying to explain them to you.

So, here's a brief summary of events: 2 years ago I wrote a request to the Pres. of Turkey asking for a personal amnesty, due to my history of mental problems (sic). We hadn't the slightest response or reply for 2 years. Then, 3 weeks ago, a paper comes from Ankara from the Minister of Justice, telling the authorities here to act upon this request and to send me to the hospital for a complete examination. O.K., so I went to Istanbul to several different hospitals several different times. Seemed to me like I was just briefly examined and since my health <u>is</u> good, I'd expect the resulting reports from these doctors to say as much. My mental state seemed to be overlooked in the series of tests I've taken so far. I'm scheduled to go back on Wed. of next week for a last visit to the hospital and to pick up my finished report. This will be sent off to Ankara to the Justice Minister—who…just happened to telegram the prison on Monday, asking where my reports were, stating that these reports were needed quickly in Ankara. Why they're needed so quickly, for what possible reason and/or motive I just don't know. But we'll wait and see…

Now, for a second piece of news. Seems the prison psychologist and I have become quite good friends. He was around last week when a paper came from Ankara, with my finished, official sentence on it. My tastik arrived with a release date of Oct. 7th, 1985… Yeah, a joke, but who's laughing. Anyway, along with this tastik paper is a request form for a transfer to another prison. This is standard procedure. When a prisoner takes his sentence, he's given a chance to change prison if he wants. Of course, some prisons are more difficult to reach than others. The severity of your sentence decreases your chances of being sent to some more informally relaxed atmosphere-type prison.

So along comes this paper for transfer request and I tell them that I want to go to an island near the Dardanelles. Everyone here tells me it's impossible for me to be sent there and not to waste my time but what the hell, can't dance, so I write this place as my first and only choice of transfer. And then…out of the blue, the psych speaks a few words about my deteriorating mental state, four years here in this stone box, and of the wonderfully refreshing atmosphere of sea and trees and real earth that I'd have on this island, and Shazzzammm! it's done and next week, after the big feast that's going on in all Muslim countries at this time, the psych says I'll be off to the island…

Now this place will be truly great since I'll be able to walk in the fields and sit by the sea with my sketch pad doing pictures. I've been doing a lot of drawing lately, really enjoy it and getting better. But here with just concrete and bars, my nervous condition doesn't allow me much of the concentration for a good picture. But down on Imrali Island Prison there are many new sights for me to sketch. I expect it will be cold there in the coming winter and that perhaps the small comforts I've acquired here will be missing but the flowers and trees should be beautiful to see for all those who'll be on the island in the Spring to see them.

I don't know for sure just what the coming of the hospital report signifies or what the special request for immediate action on them by the Minister of Justice might mean. I am putting all this to the side of my mind and am concentrating upon preparing my few things for the trip to Imrali Island. Should be there sometime in the next 2 weeks so I'll write again when I know for sure the date.

I think that I've sufficient clothing to pass the winter and if I need something it'll be easier for me to obtain it here in Istanbul rather than have you people send it all the way from New York.

I'm truly excited about going to this other prison and anxious to see trees and grass and the sea again—All prisoners work there and I guess any job will be fine with me as long as it leaves me some free time for wandering around the island drawing my pictures. I'll send you a sketch of the place after I get there.

Also…it seems 99% certain that within the next 2 months the official paperwork should be finished, whereby smugglers will receive a full 12 year amnesty like all the other categories under the law, instead of the 5 year amnesty they now have. Which would mean my release date would be Oct.7th, 1978, which is still a lot but not so bad if I can spend my time on an island where the prisoners are allowed to live like human beings instead of like sardines in this can. More on this later…

O.K. so I've spoken of judicial news but I'm thinking much about all you people. I really hope we'll be receiving some good news out of all this soon. Stay loose. Dad, I don't see any reason for calling the Fatman or his friend. Don't want the expense, don't need the connections and am reluctant to put in a new pitcher in these late innings…If I need anything from the bullpen, I'll signal. But right now it looks like fine blue sky opening over my head and life is good…

I'll be in touch soon,

Love you all

Billy

P.S. Dad, call Bone and Marc please to inform them of the situation and relay word that a letter is coming for them soon.

10-21-74, Monday

Bone, Marc, Melissa,

It seems as if the karmic balance is shifting…I've been fortunate in developing a friendship with the prison psychologist. He's newly arrived from Ankara, part of the government's effort to improve conditions for the men imprisoned in its many penal institutions.

As I've told you in my past letters, my mental condition was suffering from the harsh vibrations that surround me in this stone-steel womb. With the just-passed amnesty legislation, it looks likely that my sentence will be further reduced, leaving me only 4 more years. This piece of information is important especially when viewed with the perspective of a prison-change in mind. It seems my friend has spoken to the concerned officials and it's been agreed that I can make the move to an island prison where the conditions will be more humane and the atmosphere more conducive to my health. I'm looking forward to this very much. The island is in the Sea of Marmara, north of the Dardanelles. Name of Imrali. It'll be great to be by the sea again. I've been doing a lot of sketching lately and am anxious to have trees and sea before my eyes, to be able to draw flowers and walk in the hills. Conditions there are much better than here where we're closed up all day. Over there I'll have to work at some sort of job but on my free time I'll be able to walk about the island and have some sort of privacy with nature—be able to sketch or just sit back against a tree and gaze out at the blue sea, stretching off towards Greece and the horizon. My friend, the psychologist, believes I'll make the transfer sometime this coming week. He'll be back Wednesday from Ankara and I'm hoping to speak with him then about some timing details. A boat only goes there from Istanbul once a week so we'll have to get this together. Of course there are other boats coming there all the time for supplies and visits etcetera…era….

I'm really looking forward to going there. It will be easy to wait, quietly drawing pictures in a place like that. The Consul thinks that within a year they should have good news concerning the further reduction in my sentence and although it's winter coming on now, I'm sure Imrali will be beautiful in the spring with many flowers to see for all those who'll be there to see them…and speaking of islands, how was the surf this summer, did you do much surfing or were you too busy yachting around the Sound? But that's good experience too, a summer of sailing. I hope I'll be able to fish a little down on this island. Long time since I've fished.

Well, I'll leave you to read between the lines and ponder the implications and my love to New York and life…I'll write again immediately upon the island and tell you about the place. My regards and greetings to Mr. Phelps *[referring to Mission Impossible]*…

Love,
Crazy

11-1-74
All Souls Day

Barbara,

Paris bursting with so much life, vibrancy—sensate air and flowing energy, emotions…so many people about you, living with all their might…and you are one of them…lovers passing by, so full and aware of the moment's joy…and you are one of them…pain and sorrow and the strength that comes from weathering a storm…or a breaking on the rocks…and you are one of them. Barbara Barbara I feel you so strong. Paris bursting with so much life and your world losing its form, dissolving around you, within you *[Barbara was in a depression and life crisis]*… And once again the hollowness where love has gone—and there are no reasons for things happening the way they do, at least none that really make much sense or have much value when you're alone again…and scared…and down so low you just want to slip out from under it all, back into the waiting embrace of oblivion… Yeah, Down and downers and different shapes to the same place, no need for description, when you're there you know it… I'm feeling you so strong, Barb—I've been to Paris before. It wasn't in France then but I've been to Paris… But I'm not in Paris now and neither are you. A place maybe worth visiting for the experience but not, I repeat, <u>not</u> a place to die…

I've been wondering about you, the long silence of the summer, the turmoil of events come down in Sept. and October… Some news from here. Seems I've been fortunate in becoming friends with the newly appointed prison psychologist who's just been sent out since the Amnesty from Ankara. He's truly a conscious dude who's taken an interest in my mental condition (which you know something about) and has been helping me as best he can. By a chance (?) pattern of events, he's been able to arrange a transfer for me to an island prison where conditions are so much better, oh yes, so much better. There will be earth to walk on and trees and fields and open sky. I'll be able to walk by the sea with my sketch pad and be in contact with nature again after 4 long years of steel and stone. Right now we await only the official papers from Ankara, which are expected momentarily. Just when I go I'll believe but it does look like a balance coming to the scale… I'll write as soon as I reach the island, maybe send you my first crude sketch of the sea, the boats, etcetera…

My friend the doctor realizes I'm crazy enough to be almost sane in this insane world…and that the inmates of asylums may just be courageously mad…

Time draws near. I should go to the island within 2 weeks. Barbara, do you remember the snow-wolf running down your nights beneath the far-off Alaskan moon? And the snow is on the slopes of Switzerland. And will you hear me if I come silent across the meadows and the miles? Will you hear me if I reach out for you? Will you hear me if I reach you? Will anyone ever really hear me? Hear me now…I love you

Billy

11-1-74, Friday

Folks,

It's a cold rainy Friday, this 1st day of November. Yesterday was another Halloween. Damn, but I hate to miss Halloween; it's one of my favorite holidays.

The latest word from my psych Friend is that we're just awaiting the return of our official papers from Ankara. Upon their arrival I'll be off, seeing as how I'm paying my own boat fare down there. Am very much looking forward to leaving this prison here. Four years of stone and steel and the same gray colours. The island will be so good for my battered senses, lulled and dulled from scraping my mind on the walls…

No news about Big Mac and Company [the official Transfer Train] but it'll be so much easier waiting on the island. I don't care much about not being able to see the Consul very often. Socializing I don't need and business can be handled when and if this ballgame ever gets going. Yes, I realize the delays are technical difficulties beyond our control, but to wait until the T. govt. is together again…is just too much. Waiting on the island will make things easier. Then if in the spring the govt. comes together and I make the move under Mac's wings, O.K. Meanwhile I'll just sit here with my things all arranged, ready for the word to leave for Imrali. When I get there I'll write a more complete letter.

Mom, time to wish you a most happy birthday. I want to be home for your birthday this year but it looks like we'll have to wait a bit more now. That's all right, we're all used to waiting now. I don't say that makes it easier, but at least we're used to it. I'm feeling good and am healthy. My mental condition has improved somewhat with the news of the island transfer. I only hope you're well and smiling and still find it in you to sing in the mornings like you used to while cooking breakfast… I'll not be needing any winter clothes as I've got enough and small things like socks, etc, I'll be able to purchase from the stores and small shops in the various villages on the island. It'll be nice to walk in the fields and stand by the sea again. So nice…

Rob, I'll be writing you from the island and soon. Sorry but I keep waiting for news to send and you know what it's been like these past months…

Dad, I await a reply to my last letter: think it not necessary or wise to contact Green Lantern's man…rather wait a week or so and I'll write after the move to island…Everything holding up well, hope you're all healthy and <u>soon</u>…

Love
Billy

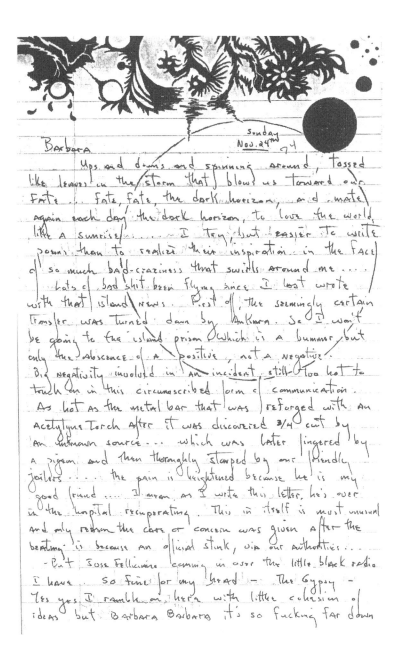

Barbara

Sunday
Nov. 24ᵗʰ '74

Ups and downs and spinning around, tossed
like leaves in the storm that blows us toward our
Fate ... Fate, fate, the dark horizon, and make
again each day the dark horizon, to love the world,
like a sunrise ...... I try, but easier to write
down than to realize their inspiration in the face
of so much bad-craziness that swirls around me ....
... Lots of bad shit been flying since I last wrote
with that island news. First off, the seemingly certain
Transfer was turned down by Ankara. So I won't
be going to the island prison (which is a bummer, but
only the absence of a positive, not a negative).
Big negativity involved in an incident, still too hot to
touch on in this circumscribed form of communication.
As hot as the metal bar that was reforged with an
acetylene torch after it was discovered 3/4 cut by
an unknown source ... which was later fingered by
a pigeon and then thoroughly stamped by our friendly
jailers .... the pain is heightened because he is my
good friend ..... I mean, as I write this letter, he's over
in the hospital recuperating. This in itself is most unusual
and only reason the care or concern was given after the
beating is because an official stink, via our authorities...
- But Jose Feliciano coming in over the little black radio
I have. So fine for my head - The Gypsy -
Yes yes I ramble on here with little cohesion of
ideas but Barbara Barbara it's so fucking far down

11-24-74, Sunday

Barbara,

Ups and downs and spinning around, tossed like leaves in the storm that blows us toward our fate…fate, fate, the dark horizon, and mate again each day the dark horizon, to love the world like a sunrise… I try, but easier to write poems than to realize their inspiration in the face of so much bad-craziness that swirls around me…

Lots of bad shit been flying since I last wrote with that island news. First off, the seemingly certain transfer was turned down by Ankara. So I won't be going to the island prison, which is a bummer but only the absence of a positive, not a negative. Big negativity involved in an incident still too hot to touch on in this circumscribed form of communication. As hot as the metal bar that was reforged with an acetylene torch after it was discovered ¾ cut by an unknown source…who was later fingered by a pigeon and then thoroughly stomped by our friendly jailers…the pain is heightened because he is my good friend *[this was a failed escape attempt with my friend Harvey, where he got caught, badly beaten, and transferred to a brutal prison far across Turkey]*… I mean as I write this letter, he's over in the hospital recuperating. This in itself is most unusual and the only reason that care or concern was given after the beating is because an official stink, via our authorities…

But some Jose Feliciano coming in over the little black radio I have. So fine for my head—"The Gypsy"— Yes, yes, I ramble on here with little cohesion of ideas but Barbara Barbara it's so fucking far down sometimes and floors keep dropping out from under us and so many levels of reality weave in and out of each other—my emotions like pingpong balls in a washing machine…

I mean, I bribed my way over to visit him yesterday and literally didn't recognize him…walked right by him…Jesus Christ! What kind of animals holding his arms and smashing in his face, knees in the balls and kicks in the spine…whew! Weird planes of space out here and fucking hell-hounds running thru the fog snuffling up emotions with their black flaring nostrils… Part of my friend's beating was because they wanted a name and he didn't give one…the hounds moving back down the tracks of the side-kick who got away…the snow-wolf on the road to Switzerland, but the fucking hounds…

Yeah, and I read your letter and it says "What shall I do with this life of mine?" And what can I say except Live it!…and love it, as hard as that may be when things crumble, fade, and pass away, even as we look at them with our unbelieving eyes…

Why worry when we can always trade tomorrow for our souls…?... Who the fuck could write shit like that?

I'll write soon,

Love

Billy

12-6-74, Friday

Folks,

It's kind of a dreary day today. Gray sky and cold. I think it just might snow. I hope so. Will be the first of the season.

I've been following the twisting path of events that may be important to our cause—that is, the break-up of the newly formed coalition here in Turkey by the Congress. I really don't have much faith left in this avenue of egress, even though I realize we may be much closer than any of us know. It just appears as if we're shuttled off to some side-track and could stand there indefinitely…if we wait, that is…

My friend, the shrink, has informed me that another attempt will be made in Ankara for a move to that island… This is mainly in light of the about-to-be finished 12-year Amnesty for smugglers, which leaves me with 3 years, 10 months, tomorrow. It's getting down there, though it is still just too much after these past 4 years. Hopefully he'll be able to pull it off this time, although I won't believe it again until I'm actually there.

I haven't heard you people speaking much of old Nana these past months. I have hesitated to ask why. I'm asking now. How is she? And how is everyone else?

It seems to me that it cannot possibly be 4 years since I've been gone. My life has a hole in it that no amount of ballast or balance can ever fill again. I truly feel like the lines of some poem I wrote long ago—"I find I'm a stranger I once might have known…"

Mom, I still don't need anything except to see your face again and even though it doesn't seem as if this will be for a long time, yet I somehow think we'll be together before too long…

Got a nice letter from Uncle Pete a while back. I've been meaning to write but you know how I'm always meaning to write everyone. Aunt Mickey still waiting for a letter from me but it is so damn difficult to extend out beyond this place, even in words and letters…

Dad, I'm in the process of getting a letter off to Mac, although news reports on my radio indicate he's been called back to D.C. I guess by New Year's we should have word on the 2d island attempt. I'll write immediately upon finding out anything.

Love to all,
Billy

12-23-74

Barb,

Hmmm, to sniff the night wind and dream. Christ! I'm getting old Barbara. My eyes are strained from the bad light and the things I've seen. I need glasses for reading. Fucking reading glasses when I used to be able to follow seagulls for as far as they could fly... I used to stare into the sunrise and saw all kinds of amazing things. Only man I knew saw more things than me was Norman and the stuff he saw made him mad as the Hatter. And now I need fucking reading glasses. And my teeth are on the rot. Some of them have rotted right up into my brain. Feels like a four year mindache, and I can't even begin to tell you about the throb in my cock. It's like electro-magnetism and I've built up such a charge this very letter may be dangerous to fertile females in a receptive state. Goddamn Barbara but I mean to tell you I got the blues—-Waaawah, Bee Brroin Boing Boing Barrranng—and I'm even learning to pluck a few strings on the guitar and they all come out blue. I get off sometimes just lying back feeling kind of sorry for myself an moanin Oh Lord! Oh Lordy! Bwank bangabrrrannnooooowwwwwnnnnnn, this road I'm on is so hard, oh yeah, it don't run smooth no more, Brraaaaooowwwnngggg!!

—The cat just leapt up onto my bed. She came in from the yard and is a little wet. She's licking off now. Sitting on my pillow quite at home. She is, literally, at home. I saw her born here in the bottom of a locker almost 4 years ago. She's been in and out, around then gone then back again. Belly getting really big now. Pregnant again. I expect within two weeks the kittens will be here. She may drop them outside somewhere but I'm thinking she's been sleeping on my bed a lot the past days...

—I'm really tired. Quit for tonight.

—But start again at 2:45 am and it seems my brain is fevered— the heat in my dreams and the heat in my loins. Ah, to be wrapped within your warm woman love...

Sunday night

Back to you again. Back to you. It's good for me, our connection. A touch of a kindred spirit, standing so small in the darkness gazing at the night. I'm capable of things now that I hadn't realized before. I can extend my sphere of perception, to focus myself into an awareness and just be…just plain drift away into the high airs of my mind and sensitivity of reception is amazing…like a blind man's hearing, so my sensitivity of feeling… Hmmm… Shit, so hard to explain things with words… On the scorpion's tail…

Christmas Eve

Still haven't gotten this off. Moody tonight. Thinking of you. Thinking of people I love. I got a letter from my mother. She doesn't write too often because we were never into words, just smiles and laughs and love. Remembrances of things past. She says, "Here I am remembering about long ago. They say that's a sign of growing old… I'm fine, still the same, life goes on even with a little heartache everyday for my oldest child so far away." Jesus, that tears me up. And the cat has one kitten in the box on my bed. More to come. I felt her spasms with my hand on her belly. What is it? Days within years, wombs within wombs, kittens to cats to kittens and it continues…and the same God that made the day made the night…

For my friend, it's much harder. He wrote last week and is out in the sticks in an old rathole of a prison in eastern Turkey. The only foreigner. The only non-believer. It's heavy. But so is he so I hope for him as I hope for me as I hope for us…powerful thing, hope, I'm thinking it's some kind of energy channel, God's glittering eyes in the darkness…

Dec 25th

Still only one kitten but her belly promises more in the fullness of time. Feel good about this Christmas night birth. Read significance into such things… Have to…

Christmas card yesterday from Marc—

"Wishing you love…the heart of Christmas..."

from him to me and now from me to you—wishing you love Barb, for being there, for being Barbara, for being you, for being, for all reasons, for no fucking reason at all...

Yeah, a lucky New Year... I can dig it...

Love

Billy

1975

Folks,

Well, it's a rainy Wednesday morning and already 8 days into 1975. I'm sitting at the table downstairs because, as usual, the heaters aren't working and it's purty chilly. Our tea-stove is down here so it's better than the upstairs room. Actually, I don't feel the cold much any more. With my long underwear and a sweater beneath my jacket it's not so bad. The new people are all freezing. Soft on the outside, but they'll get used to it after a while.

Still no news about anything. This AF I've been talking about is still being worked out in some committee somewhere. What it is: the Amnesty in May granted 12 years to all categories of crime except the smugglers. But civil liberty-type groups have been protesting the inequality of granting 12 years to everyone else and only 5 years to the smugglers. So it is almost certain now that an additional 7 years will be granted to us. Informed people here say it is a 100% certainty. We are waiting daily for the official announcement. It is important to me. My release date is now Oct. 7th, 1985. But with the additional 7 years my release date would be Oct. 7th, 1978. This means my chances for going to a better prison, like that island I mentioned before, are much better. We're waiting for AF to be official then my shrink friend will petition Ankara for the transfer. I'm also going to contact Mac and see what he can do to help from this end. It would be good if I could go to the island prison for the remainder of my sentence. It isn't certain but there's a good chance that if Ecevit is elected he will grant a small Amnesty. This would be good for me. So I'm waiting for the 7 year addition before requesting another transfer. When the 7 years comes, I hope my request will be granted…

Anyway, that's the legal scene.

From the sound of it, the family's been taking a beating this winter. Mom's accident and now Dad with a 2 week cold. Hey! You people have to be careful with your health, it's important. You're the only parents I have!

Rob's books arrived and Erdogan *[a Turkish employee at the American Consulate]* brought them out special on New Year's Eve. He's a good man to have on our side over here.

Mom, I was really happy to get your letter. For someone who doesn't have a way with words, you sure said a lot. Jesus! it tears me up to think about the hurt you all have taken from this madness. How do I make this up to you???

The holiday party at our house sounded like quite a bash. I can imagine Aunt Mickey and Aunt Eileen smashed but it stretches my mind to the limits to hear that Aunt Mary was the one trying to sober people up. The world really must be changing out there while I'm in here…

You understand when I say I don't need the Christmas gift from Br. Gerald *[the Franciscan brother who tutored me for my SAT tests]* and company but I certainly do appreciate it. Times are hard all over. In here the price of everything has inflated so that if I weren't reading about the world economic situation I just wouldn't believe the prices of food. Everything has doubled or tripled and some things just can't be found for any price. It's getting heavy. I worry about the world.

Look, it may sound like a load of bull, but it really is hard to write letters. I've insulated myself, kind of sealed off from the outside and it's hard to extend out with letters to all those people I should write. Explain this if you can.

I went to the doctor today. I'll be going for an eye test soon. I definitely need reading glasses. Me, who used to be able to watch seagulls until they flew off the end of the earth. Yes, yes, the price to pay for the way I live…

I've been corresponding regular with Barbara. She's working in a ski shop in Switzerland to make ends meet—up on the slopes whenever she can get away. If I ever leave I have to see what her plans are. Morocco for a few weeks, months… I need some place quiet and sunshine for my mind. The energy excitement of N.Y. would be hard to jump into directly from here…

O.K. so that's about all there is to say at this point. I expect to hear soon about the finalization of this AF—and then the transfer request. I'll keep you informed.

Love to all
Billy

1-12-75

Marc,

Got your Christmas card. Thanks. It expresses my sentiment exactly. But there wasn't any mention of receiving my Dec.11th letter. Which you must have received by now. There was a request in there for fifty of Miss Lucille's finest little mindblowers. Perhaps the import of this request wasn't made clear in the jumbled blabbering that surrounded it. So I'll lay it out in more detail now—able to send this via trusted courier and avoid the feeble-minded but vaguely capable prison censors.

Legal situation: 30 year sentence

<u>-10 years good behavior</u>

20 years to serve

Now this 20 is further reduced by the Amnesty of May 1974. Currently I'm reduced by 5 years—<u>but</u> a further reduction is pending, certain, only waiting official publication. This would grant me another 7 years—total 12 years of Amnesty:

20

<u>-12</u>

8 years to serve

I've been here 4 yrs 2 months 23 days, which means more than 3 fucking years more before release date of Oct. 7th 1978—

So....................What does the future legal scene look like?

1. The American Govt. action you are aware of appears to have reached some kind of a snag, perhaps due to the governmental turmoil here in The Big Gobbler. So this line of future possibility seems certain to be tied up until the political situation here is straightened out. I cannot begin to explain the absurdity of the political here but it does not look promising for any solution within the near future…

2. <u>But</u>…if Allah is Great <u>and</u> a certain politician wins, <u>maybe</u> he'll grant a small 5 year amnesty to celebrate his election. This is customary though not overly common practice. This would be just fine with me, I'd be out… I rate it somewhere between the

ruptured monkey rollerskating thru that buffalo herd and Richard Nixon's chances to become Pope...

3. After (Feb.6th) the 12 year reduction takes affect, my chances to request another transfer to that island prison will be much better. Perhaps I'll be able to go there with just 3 years left to a 30 year sentence. I am currently figuring this possibility line very strongly into my plans. I am going to keep it in the first slot because if it comes across then everything else is unimportant. The island is where it's at—definitely. So I'm holding up everything until I know yes or no on the island transfer...But...

4. If the island transfer doesn't work then I'm going to be transferred to another prison on the eastern border of Turkey, just near Iran. The location is important only in that it takes almost 3 days to get there by bus and train. Quite a long time of traveling for me and the two soldiers who'll accompany me. It will be a pleasant trip for me. Able to see the country and soak up all the new impressions that will present themselves to my dehydrated senses. It will be enjoyable to talk with the soldiers along the way. My Turkish isn't bad now and I find I get along really well with Turk soldiers. They're just dudes who've been drafted—they don't like it either. I think it'll be an interesting trip for them also. Ten of Miss Lucy's finest *[LSD, of course]* for each should do the trick. From there it's just run rabbit run and quick down into one of the many holes already established, only to reappear, presto chango, a brown fox, a quick brown fox leaping over the garden wall...

I've gone over this in theory and in dress rehearsal several times. I am not just jumping off the wall into the pit again. I found out what happens when you don't look to see where the rhino is and what his habits are. A tranquilizer gun would do the trick better but there is a problem of logistics and administration. Those film-like window-panes are just perfect size and oh so effective. I'm asking you for fifty to be sure. I'll arrange it in different forms and shapes to meet the variations in situation application. I want you to send two letters. Cover them with 3 or 4 airmail insignias. Lick the edges of one so that outer border is wet and middle part is dry. Place a goodly number of those panes in the dry part and seal onto letter. I think you'll see that fifty fit very easily between two or three insignias. Twenty five to a letter would be cool. Don't worry, this is a tried and proved method. Use bogus names and give my home address as return. Send these letters off to me immediately, if not sooner. I want to be able to check this most important item off my list.

I'm sorry to hit you for this but it's only you and Bone who I can rely on to get this together. I'd be truly happy if some surprise comes before this madness is necessary, but I have come to believe that some kinetic action is needed. And I mean it's more than time. I just cannot and will not wait anymore for this situation to resolve itself. I mean, I was 23 back then and I'm 27 now, and I need fucking reading glasses, my eyes are strained from the light in here and all the things I've seen. My teeth are rotting right up into my brain. My dick aches to be wrapped inside some sweet woman warmth.

I don't want to hear anything about taking it easy and wait or anymore of that shit. I'm taking it easy or I'm taking it hard but I'm going to take it. So now don't tell me you can't find any windowpanes in N.Y.C. Mickey Finn would be better but its transportation problems. Write me soon with news from there and get on the stick!!

Love to all
Billy

1-22-75

Barbara,

Wednesday in the afternoon. A chill grayness to the day, drizzling…and a damp cold so still and thick I can sit here on my bed and fog the air with my breath…

The only two heaters we had didn't work very well of often but it doesn't matter now since the T's came in and removed them 10 days ago, under the shabby pretext that "all new modern-pipe radiators were to be installed, forthwith…", of course, nothing has begun as of this writing and meanwhile we freeze our balls off—I mean, goddamn! but it's cold waking in the morning. Some days I'm so fucked up with the chill that's settled in my bones during the night that I come up out of bed at 6 a.m. exercising like some spastic Eskimo who fell thru the ice—yoga and sit-ups and pushups and jumping-a-jacks until the ice-cold morning water comes spurting out the spout into the downstairs sink and just for the sheer masochistic fuck of it I take a bath. In a way it's the thing to do because for the rest of the day I can only get warmer. This slow creeping kind of cold is bad news. Better to get it all over at once and then try to inner-fuel my way thru the rest of the day.

Yes, that was quite a letter I received from you last week. You talk of Ronnie Foley and I think of Diane Krauer [Diane was high school romance, first sex and heartbreak… Aah, love…]. You speak of it being hard to grasp the passage of time—Ronnie's two children. Yes, yes. And what to say except that the kitten is 4 weeks old today. His eyes are open for 10 days now and he's beginning to gain the kitten coordination that I find so irresistible to watch. He falls off the bed quite frequently now but it doesn't seem to hurt him any because he just keeps doing it. Maybe on purpose as being the only way to the floor and all that curiosity-space beyond. The mother's become a cranky bitch who yowls around at night and must be from all signs hot in heat again. But we put up with her cause she did such a good job having the kitten and feeds him so often that he's just a fat ball of fluffy energy when not sleeping. My time perspective is sharpened or distorted (I'm not sure which) when I see the two of them together on my bed and remember this same mother cat asleep as a kitten on another bed almost 4 years before. Somewhere in some notes somewhere I've got down something like—"cats within kittens, wombs within wombs, days within weeks within years, all growing toward the fullness of infinity"—or some such pap. Just those frisky little symbol-sounds that can make pretentious even your most precious experiences...

Night now: took a hot bath an hour ago at 7:30. I rate it the most sensual experience of the week. Every 7 days a different group of us strip down to our underwear (freakily forbidden by guards to go naked here—"creates problems" they say) and gather shivering around the sink in the downstairs "kitchen" to await the hot water. It runs about an hour when it runs. If it runs. Kind of hit and miss— if your night isn't hot, then it's another week wait (if you wait). But when it comes, oh my, so fine to feel that hot water steaming over my goosebumped flesh. And to wash my hair. So very dirty and smelly you get, and it is here! I get clean from the bath, from soaping up and dipping my pitcher into the water then splashing it over myself. The room fills with steam and maybe you wash a back or someone washes yours. Feels good to touch other human beings. Wish I could find a way to combine the emotional power, the high-voltage connection (what I call "God's Hardon") with the physical realities of this scene. I mean to say that titillation is no longer the aim of my social endeavors. I would love with the knowledge of...what to say? I don't know. Before, outside, before I learned whatever it is I learned, I loved fully, as fully as I was able. It was good and so fine and I fucked everything that moved and grooved my way—women, girls, a neighbor's pet boxer when I was 12 years old, fish, goats, night creatures, mythological animals and even a pale Englishboy on a night-train through France...but somehow I feel I've expanded my capacity to love and I would love with an intensity of heightened awareness—God's Hardon...

A woman is needed. So badly needed. Complementing vibrations, awareness, passing souls across thru our eyes...

Thursday morning

Yes, newspaper articles continue. Kind of difficult to grasp the meaning of all this. The people-response has been very encouraging. Nice to feel all that concentration just when you feel so very far down and o such a long way out…but I'm not sure what's going to develop other than that which does… Just get it on, get it on, patience and points of diminishing returns…

Beth *[Beth had traveled Europe with Barbara, sharing the fullness of life, breaking her heart…]* has sent several letters and postcards from some really outrageous places. When she left here that day, telling me of her plans to travel alone to Baghdad and points East, I blessed her for being such a brave but foolish young woman. I mean, that area of the world is not known for being overly hospitable to pale blond Jewish ladies out exploring by themselves. But I did seem to detect some signs of the independent strength she possesses—and her travels have indicated the same. Last letter was from Israel address:

I haven't written yet but will soon.

Keep hoping to have a different return address to add to the back of my letters…

Got to go. I'll be writing in coming days. News is expected from several fronts…as usual…

I breathe your mountainair, so clear, so clear…

I love you, Barbara

Billy

2-26-75

Barb,

Just words to you out of emptiness...lonely Wednesday evening, long gray day of rain and heavy plopping snowflakes that lost their form and their magic the moment they met the wet cement-stone of the courtyard...no transforming power in them...sterile...cold stone sorrow and sad rain... I didn't even go out in the yard today, chill stone dreariness seeping out of the sky today, feeling the pull of the full moon today, kind of down but dangerous and feeling mean... Edgy with people and balancing with difficulty... Managing, but the effort leaves me feeling slightly drained. It shouldn't be like this but centers are definitely shifting out of alignment lately as events move toward what must be a climax...of one sort or another...

Thursday morning

The temperature dropped in the night and a white wonder covering everything this still snowy morning. Fine, it brings me up...my moods, the flowing emotional tide within me, around me...

Had a visit last week from two nice young dudes from the Children of God. They're into something really strong for them... it shows on their faces and in their eyes. One curly-haired kid, 19, from California, with a cherubim-face who hardly spoke at all, just stared at me through the glass panels in that cramped little cabin. It was amazing—the other guy and I rapped Jesus, life, drugs, high and low, we flowed across to each other in our ideas—and all the while this beautiful freak, stoned-out on God, just beaming at me, and I'm feeling him all warmth and love with me beaming back and the energy charging up so that after a while we just stood there gazing thru the glass in silence, smiling, slowbreathing, filling on each other... I remember you moving backward out the same cabin and our eyes fixed on that line that still holds us...

On the bed behind me, behind a mutually acceptable separation curtain, sleeps a 44 year old Iranian who was busted 1 ½ years ago with 650 k's in a truck. Extremely aggressive individual, quite clever and versed in prison life, with the emotional maturity of a 12 year old boy. Also been a heroin addict the last 15 years now... He keeps two young French junkchildren on a string of paracodeine and hops that he cops from the doctor and dope that he's dealing in progressively greater quantities until now he's come to control this entire left half of the prison as his territory. As his business influence has grown so has his ability to extend his kinky head activities without fear of legal retribution (8 yrs. in T. Land for homosexuality) because he's big time in the dope hierarchy and cooperation is obtainable... He and the French kids have a working arrangement—head for head, head for ass, he keeps them stoned and they let him run his "slave, suck my cock!" trip... It's a weird show to have running behind me every day. It's a delicately balanced relationship I have with this guy...of necessity must relate to people on their own terms in here...me to his and he to mine...after we understood each other's position on certain matters, a friendship of sorts has developed...but it's strange goings on...all sorts of untuned vibrations and kinky craziness. I've tasted this scene before and while finding it physically gratifying it seemed somehow disharmonious, an emotional dissonance that I've come to attribute to a lack of love...like a man can only approach a woman or another man physically in terms of buyer-seller, prostitute-customer, master-slave, the dominator and the dominated...a sad affair, indeed, for while love must be paid for, it can't be bought... It comes back to God's Hard-on, whether it be in your pussy, in your ass, or in your mouth...or in someone else who is aware that, literally, they're fucking and they are, God—well, this is where it feels like it's at, for me at least... (And touch the erogenous zones of God with a smile)...

I mean physical loving without emotional sincerity doesn't feel right... I'm sorry for the French kids that they so readily sell parts of themselves for their dope and for the Iranian that he has to buy what should be given freely and completely or not at all...

Ah, yes, and as long as I'm so far out here in this direction, do you know that I'm limber enough from the Yoga that I can close the curtain on my bed and roll up and actually mouth my own cock...? Well, I can, can take in the head and a bit of the shaft...enough...but if my spine were looser or my cock longer...anyway, it's as sincere as I can be at the moment... Can't, don't want to, maybe just afraid to form those emotional bonds here again... Looking too hard to be Out, feeling the Outside too hard now... Wondering about you, Woman...feel such affinity to your words and to your very life... And when you speak about us living together, living and loving together as we live and love separately now, Yes I understand about what it means to live with someone, but how can I answer your question, as it's my question also—will it be the same when I get out? You're asking if our love will grow. I don't know...don't know...

You asked for another photo but don't seem to have any around at moment, sent a lot of junk out to consul etc. a while back, just to be sure of seeing it again someday, but sending this sketch of another self-portrait I did last year...I like it...

Wednesday, March 5th

It's a week since I began this. The mailing delay was due to news expectations which haven't come as yet. I expected a consul visit with a definitive answer on my isle transfer request—but, alas, they came out yesterday with some mumble-fumble which amounts to more time needed before decision can be received. How much time, we don't know. They don't know, that is. I know how long I'm waiting for the answer. Like going around the Zoo in one of those sightseeing trains or running the Rhino pit... The train is grooved and smooth but sometimes you don't get a ticket and got to use the feet... I don't know about train-time now until that request comes back but I know about feet-time and sniff sniff Mr. Sandman sprinkle your magic dust on those Rhinos one time for me...

Feeling you Barbara,
Billy

4-8-75

Folks,

Thanks for all the birthday cards. Nana, made me laugh…

Items: received the Dostoyevsky books and the underwear. Await the pants; the guys at the Consul will bring them out soon as they arrive. They've really been friends for me, and have done all they can and then some to help…

As for Mac and the nut reports…I'm been speaking with Phil Amerman [from the Consulate] and coordinating our request thru him and the Ankara people—our reply from Ankara should be coming in (?) one of these days. Just when, I can't say, you know about these things here in this country. But hopefully it will be soon. After the reply then we can talk about Pilgrim State plan … Phil and people here seem to agree with me the P.S. wouldn't enhance my chances for a transfer so I just told them to wait with all that stuff—I really don't think it has much chance of success—especially since a paper came for me from Ankara last week. It was an official reply re my 1972 request for a personal pardon due to my deteriorating mental condition. It said that the Justice Dept., after examining the reports from the various hospitals I went to last October, find that I am not sufficiently ill to be included under Turkish law in the category allowing for pardon due to mental reasons… So, this would appear to be a big negative among the files and I think would make a P.S. plan less feasible…(even though there were no mental examinations per se at these hospitals)…but right now I'm just waiting for a reply…the people here including Mace [the current Consul] know that I vetoed the P.S plan in favor of an isle request… I've left the P.S. open, awaiting results, but they, as I, felt that P.S. has little chance unless someone has a string attached at this end or Ankara end…and after promptings from me and inquires from here, we've yet to receive any confirmation that there is any kind of string. This may be due to understandable discretion on the part of Mac etc but I'm not keen on it. So if you want to get past the need for whitelies just tell them the truth of the moment, i.e., I'm waiting for a reply on my transfer request and refuse to become crazy until then...

I hope to hear some news soon so I'll be in touch again shortly... Thanks, people, your love and strength get me through the days, the days...

Love, Billy

P.S. Please mail these 2 included letters for a deceiving friend...

P.P.S. Did you get the drawing of me in last letter?

5-14-75, Wednesday

Folks,

So…some news of import, for a change… The official confirmation has been printed and finally finished; my official release date is now October 7, 1978, due to the additional 7 years amnesty… And on Tuesday, Dave was out to congratulate me, for what it's worth, to have 3 ½ more years remaining now… I asked about the transfer news and he told me of the most recent reply from the T official contacted in Ankara, which is, that it isn't just a simple matter of Yes or No but that it must be approved in different places and that's where it is now…but Dave said indications from the official were good. In fact, he told the Consul people (in advance) that the AF finalities were just a few days off and that after my sentence was officially 3 ½ instead of 10 ½ the decision would be coming forthwith…

So, anyway, I am more optimistic now than I have been in quite a while…it will be very good on my eyes to see green again and for my feet to walk on the earth instead of this concrete stone. I'm looking forward to working outdoors in nature and hope the decision comes soon because it's Springtime and Summer's coming…I can feel it in the air of my dreams… I wake in the early mornings like I was going out fishing or something… Certainly would like to be doing farmwork on Imrali this summer…really would enjoy the earth and the sun… Let's see, should be some sort of decision soon… The Pilgrim is always waiting in the wings…

Package received. Thanks. I mentioned lots of actual news in my last letter (May 1st?) but your May7th letter didn't mention receiving this one…our communication gap again… Oh, yes, and I think it may not be time or place to make any list of clothing or pants or baseball glove etc. that I may need—better to wait and after I go I'll write to tell you what I may need in the way of clothes, shoes, and those obvious etceteras…

Yes, O.K., that's all for now…I'll be writing soon as news comes…

Love to All,

Billy

P.S. Ah, yes, and a Happy Mothers' Day to Mom and Nana, even though every day I think about you…

5/25/75, Thursday

Barbara,

The sound of your name and a rising heat in my loins as I lie here on my bunk in the late afternoon, sort of really-summer sweating and thinking how fine it would be if you and I could touch our bodies like we touch our minds...just to love so free and loose and easy beneath the sun of some blue mountain sky... I'm thinking we could fill each other to overflowing with such a fresh sort of happiness that who knows how long it might last—a moment, a month, more, much more...

But again, all these foolish little words and such a distance across to something more than paper reality. No, that's not quite correct, because I feel you so strong in between the letters, between the words, that our distance is only measured in kilometers...

Yes, to need a voice... I wonder if I'll ever hear you breathing there beside me in the softness of the morning before the dawn and watch you come awake, saying Mmmmmmmm...

Prison, what to say about it after all this time? Strange little things, small favors and joys to balance the ugly madness... Like today, I don't know why or from where, maybe some epidemic of hoof n' mouth disease or some donkeys on the track when the train came thru, but anyway they came around to the doors of the block today selling fucking chop-meat! I mean, real hamburger meat, which we never see here like this, it blew us out, about $2.50/ kilo, but so very very fine to fry it up with some egg and onions and a little garlic then some sort of strong-sauced Italian concoction mixed up by two friends... Ah, yes, how easily satisfied I am, just fill my belly and tickle my balls and I'm all right for at least a couple of hours...

News of import perhaps... Since I last wrote you the legal scene seems to have taken a turn for the better... On April 10th my transfer request was accepted in Ankara and the word was that an answer would be coming soon after my sentence was officially reduced to Oct 7th, 1978 release date... Well, on May 12th the reduction was finally made official and even though I haven't heard yet, I and the consul people are rather optimistic about chances... I'll write you immediately when I hear...

    B

6-6-75, Sunday

Folks,

So what to say about this situation. I just don't know except that perhaps waiting will provide an answer… And then, again, perhaps it won't…

Phil was out from the Consul this week. No news from them on the isle; though I truly don't expect them to know anything until notified by Ankara, either thru the Turkish Authorities or the Embassy Staff… I've been pressing them to phone whoever it's necessary to phone and to find a reason for the seemingly excessive wait on this request. I realize, as do they, that we're dealing with red tape of a sort and I also realize that signs seem to be good so far for approval and that perhaps we shouldn't press too hard… But…I also feel like someone is bullshitting me here about this thing… I mean first it was the end of April, and then soon after the AF (May 12th) and now it's the 3d of June. When I ask Phil if they've called the dude in Ankara since our previous visit May 13th he says no and when I ask why it seems to me that there are things left unsaid in our conversation… It's very possible I'm just misinterpreting the picture due to a focus problem, but I've told him to get in touch with Ankara and find out what's happening, because if I don't get a change of climate soon I fear for my equilibrium, I mean I feel on the edge of a P.S. attack… But let's just wait and stay calm a little while longer… I feel for something to come about soon…

And what about sending me some of those new articles from *Newsday*, etc. I'm interested in seeing what is written about this from the outside-perspective… And yes, it is partly by ear, but a well-tuned ear with a sound system…

My friend B.F. *[Ben Franklin]* isn't what he used to be back in the beginning of '74 but he's doing all right and will suffice, I believe…

The sports season is here but I don't know about the baseball results. Actually thinking about my old Phelps Lane job *[lifeguard, swimming, island prison…]* and along these lines as the heat here comes up to summer temperatures... And Bobby tells me about bicycling thru the City...I'd really like that... Later will be more time for this discussion, thinking in terms of individual events rather than medley at this point...

And I hear from Bone he's being married sometime this Autumn... Now that's something I just have to see!!... *Inshallah*...

There are strange rumors about a foreign minister's conference in Strasbourg last week...some news article on the radio here about a revision of foreign-prisoner situation... You people know anything about this? Just some more wind, I'm thinking, but perhaps...

And what about writing a friendly letter to Mac to find out what's happening here with this request... I mean, get it on, get it on....

I love you all, don't worry, everything will be fine, in time, in time...

Billy

P.S. Tell me what date you get this letter.

7-8-75, Tuesday

Barbara,

Forgive me for not writing. It's been a changing time. And now, after many a tangled fate-line, it seems I'm on my way to another prison. It's an island prison named Imrali. The physical surroundings will be so soothing to me. At present there aren't any other foreign prisoners so I will be quite alone. But I've learned about loneliness. It's not something new to me now. The island is difficult to reach so outside visits will be few and far between. But the physical and mental isolation are a small price to pay for the privilege of walking once more on real earth and gazing at the sea. To feel grass and smell flowers, to touch my hand to the skin of a living tree...yes, worth whatever the cost...

The boat leaves every Friday. It seems as if I'll leave next week, when they have sufficient soldiers to accompany me, dangerous criminal that I am.

Anyway, I'm excited about the change. Go with the flow and let's see where this leads...

There's rumor of an INFAZ reduction in the wind. This is the good behavior time automatically subtracted from our sentences. So my 30 years is automatically reduced by 1/3d, i.e., 10 years. Now there's talk of an INFAZ increase to ½ which means a 15 year reduction from my 30 year sentence, which would mean I'd be free if and when this plan was adopted.

Unfortunately, it must be approved by the Turkish Parliament and they've just gone out on vacation until mid-October. So even if the rumors are true, nothing can possibly happen until then. Word here is that the ½ INFAZ will be finished before Christmas. Yes, would be nice... A new year...

Night

And if all life is sacred, how can I chase these flies from the string beside my bed...or the cockroaches off the bread in my locker...or slap the mosquito that lands on my face in the night? Drink my blood but leave no poison, I think to him... And softly he probes down within my body, sucking life from me, feeding off me as I feed off other life forms...and who am I to deny him this little thing? This tiny sip of me which will fill him for so many hours, sustain him perhaps like a smile or just the smallest act of human kindness sustains the soul of a lonely love-starved man...

Wed.

Strange the reaction in me when I read that you'll be leaving for home on the 24th... I'd like you to visit my family if you can. The personal contact is so important and if anyone can touch them for me, it's you...

And about Marc...I just don't know what to say... It's been 3-4 months since I heard from him... He doesn't forget but I think there's a feeling of, yeah, just a feeling from him that holds him back from writing... My letter today should draw a response... I miss him, his letters and his presence are food for me... His long silence is an absence that makes me sad, thoughts and memories of Norman gone like so many of our yesterdays...

Have a good trip, Barb,

I love you woman

Billy

7-9-75

Marc,

I wrote you on the 30th of March. I wrote you on the 19th of May. I wrote you on the 6th of June. And now I'm writing you again…

From the response I've received, I may as well be writing to Norman.

The request I made and your inability to fulfill it seem to have so daunted you that you hesitate to even write me a letter…Jesus Christ! Don't you know that I need your words and the spirit that flows thru them more than any fucking request. I mean, it hurts, Marc.

And now I'm leaving for another prison. It's an island-prison, name of Imrali, located in the Marmara Sea. There are both advantages and disadvantages in going there. Since it is an island and rather difficult to get to, I'll be out of contact with Consul people or other visitors, who help by their trips out here. And since there are no other foreigners on this island, I'll be rather alone in my head. But loneliness is something I've learned about. It doesn't touch me so now. The physical and mental isolation of this new place are really a small price to pay for being out of this concrete cage I've been in these past 5 years. The island is situated so that prisoners can work out in the fields and be in contact with nature. I'll be able to touch real earth again and smell flowers after so long surrounded by cold stone. I'll be able to walk by the sea and sit alone on the grass of some little hill, feel the clean sea breeze on my face. Yes, the isolation will be a small price to pay for such soul-soothing experiences.

All prisoners on this island are required to work. Just what sort of job I'll receive, I don't know. But I'm sure it will be all right with me. Just so I can touch nature again and maybe even swim in the sea. Yowwwww! to swim again after so long. The most water we have here is once a week a bath, washing with a pitcher from a sink.

And the trip down there should be such a treat. A boat ride. Imagine! A boat ride out on the open sea for a couple of hours, with sky and sun and seagulls and movement! Movement after so long sedentary. Yes, I'm looking forward to it. My request would fit in quite well right here at this point but it's too late now. The boat leaves every Friday and I'll probably be off next week, though maybe this Friday if they can find the soldiers necessary to accompany such a dangerous criminal like myself.

Anyway, I just wanted write and tell you what's happening. Bone wrote and tells me not only is he getting married but quitting his job and maybe buying Real Fucking Chili back in Milwaukee *[Real Chili, our favorite late night Mexican joint in Milwaukee, was the scene of many bizarre displays of collegiate behavior at its most perverse]*. Wow! <u>That</u> blows my mind.

And what about you? What's going on?

I'll write again from the island. Write me. Same address, friends here will forward.

Love to all and everyone and to you…

Billy

7-14-75

Folks,

So here I am on Imrali island, writing you a letter in the clear blue open air. I'm so amazed at the nature around me. Tall trees in the wind. White-capped water. A horseshoe-shaped bay, and a lavender mist at the far horizon where the deep blue of the Marmara meets the Asian hills.

This prison is just a handful of old buildings that might have been a village, time past. Dormitory-style rooms with creaky wooden floors and metal bunk beds. A bit dirty but that doesn't bother me anymore. I'm in a room with about thirty other guys. The atmosphere is much different from Sagmalcilar. All the prisoners have small time remaining and fairly good records...not much of the fighting and stabbing that was routine in the other place.

The first day I arrived here was Friday, our free day. Do you believe it? I'm swimming in the sea! I mean, after five years of washing from a sink, I'm swimming in the sea. It's just amazing.

I'm working in the conserve factory, which is just an old building fitted out to process the many varieties of fruit grown here and elsewhere. First workday we picked the stems off of 40 million strawberries. I couldn't believe it. All the strawberries I could eat. After three hours of cleaning and wolfing them down I had to run to the toilet. But it was fantastic. Now I work at a machine, doing monkey-work, making the metal covers for the cans we use for the conserve. It's all right.

I'm sunburned, not much but just enough to make me feel good. Laid on the beach yesterday and today from twelve until two. I don't eat the lunch offered. We're allowed to walk around the island, and so I go far off down the beach, up one leg of the bay where I'm alone. Just me and the sea. It's so fine to be alone, to be away from people for the first time in five years, to lie still in the sunshine and listen to the gulls.

They say the winters here are really cold. But I can stand anything now. It will be a small price to pay for the freedom of movement, not to mention opportunity…more about this in coming letters when I've become better acquainted with the place.

I still can't get over that picture of the whole clan together. Nana looks like she's getting younger all the time. And Dad, it struck me as so strange to hear that you had to prune the trees in the backyard to let the sun in. I thought "What trees?" and then remembered that trees grow a lot in five years. Like people.

Barbara should be back in North Babylon on July 24. I've asked her to stop by for a visit. She should be able to tell you a lot from the letters I've written her. I don't really know what's to become of my life in the days to come. But Barbara's gotten me through some of the hardest times. I wonder what could be if we could be together in the good times. Seems as if I've learned something about loving and giving while in here…too late for Kathleen but Barbara, yes, Barbara, who knows? I'll write next week when things have developed a bit more. Don't worry…

Love to you all,
Billy

8-2-75, Saturday

Folks,

Received your July 23d and 25th letters. Yes, we're all happy about this island. It's truly a godsend for me. My nose is sunburned and I'm feeling just healthy as can be, considering all circumstances. Mike Griffith was here last Friday, July 25th. A very nice visit. He was out again on Tuesday July29th and the P.E. *[prisoner exchange treaty]* news has been laid on me. Mike's optimism is high and while I believe the hearts of all involved, it just seems like I've heard this song before. But anyway, let's hope for the best. He was going back to see Mr. Mac again on Wed. and then off to Sardinia etc. for business-pleasure. I like him, he's a good friend and I think a quite competent man to have behind us. If this thing comes off it will be a lot of this credit. But truly, I have my doubts, especially considering the embargo situation and Turk-U.S. relations...it just doesn't seem the time for favors to be extended...

And Dad, while it's true that Lew the Lip might be a bit forward in his tactics, it must be admitted that he's won a lot of ball games... And to extend analogies, I feel rather like Willie Mays on 3d rather than on 1st... And you know what Willie used to do from there *[Willie Mays used to steal home, a rare and amazing feat]*...let's just see how the game progresses... No sense in being tagged out now, but runs don't count unless they cross the plate...

My last letter was mailed on the 19th so if you got it on the 24th that's not bad... This one will go out with a friend on Tuesday and should be in the mail by Wed. August 6th... Let me know when you receive it... And the mail situation here is pretty good... It's accepted practice to send out mail uncensored, with friends who visit or guys going free...and I received your 25th letter unopened but there is supposed to be a control...that means they'll open it usually to inspect for contraband but no one here reads English so it doesn't matter. But nevertheless, our standard euphemisms and sloppy handwritings should continue just for the hell of it...

I took Mike on a little tour of the place on Tuesday and I guess he's told you all about it by now. The food's not much but I'm finding the underground markets and learning the ropes so it's getting better. He was impressed with the atmosphere of my living quarters, especially the toilets...but, in truth, the place had just been cleaned because the Minister of Justice was here on Sunday July 27th for a visit and the whole place got a once over... But even after the cleaning the toilet is something else... And ask Mike about toilet paper and the flies...they blew his mind...

Things I need for winter, yes, and it should be a <u>really</u> cold winter here. Let's try this list:

- Thermal underwear
- Sweat suit
- 2 Flannel shirts
- 1 pair corduroy pants (one is enough)
- My old Navy pea coat if it's still around
- One wool ski-hat (dark blue or black)

That's about all I really think I'll need from your end in the way of winter clothing. Sweaters and socks I have and nothing else seems necessary at this time. Actually, I'm really not planning on actually using any of this stuff but it's better to be prepared. And the package may take a while to get here. Best method I think will be to leave my name off it entirely. Rather mail it to David Bloch at the American Consulate. I've written him about this and expect an answer soon to confirm this method. You won't be mailing your package for a couple of weeks at least, so I'll get a letter to you before that. So in my next letter I'll let you know for sure about this.

Also, Dad, there's a guy here who's become a friend and an influential one at that since he works in the Public Prosecutor's office here on the island he has a relative living in xxxxx. She's been there 12 years now and speaks good English. His problem is that anything she might send him is taxed 100% by the Turks when it arrives. A favor to him would be if we could include some things for him in our package. He's written his wife and she'll get these items together. She'll also be expecting a telephone call from you so that the two of you can best arrange getting together the items. I hope this isn't a big inconvenience for you but he tells me things won't weigh much—just some clothes and a tape recorder. They'd tax him a fortune here if it came regular post. I'd like to help him out so if you can call this number xxxxxx and arrange contact with his wife I'd appreciate it. Maybe wait a week or so and be sure she's gotten his letter explaining the situation...

Yes, I'm not surprised Peg and Rob didn't guess my name as the one who'd been swimming and sunburned. I still don't believe it and I'm in the water every day. And Mom, have no fear, any shark that gets close enough I'll bite and eat right there in the water. I like fish.

Anyway, some sort of interesting news should be forthcoming before the summer is out. Let's wait and see.

And a most Happy Birthday, Dad, just in case the mail gets fouled up before the 24th. For sure we'll go out for a beer on your next.

So much love to all folks, the sun is shining, we're alive and life is so fine...

Billy

P.S. Has Barbara been over?

8-12-75
Tuesday
5:30a.m.

Marc,

Yes, a letter from you, finally. And such a fine letter, too. Now, was that so difficult? Anyway, it made me feel your mood and the strength of your badger-like tenacity. Yes, persist, by all means... Like old Luke says, "Sometimes nothin' is a real cool hand"... Shuffle and double-clutch and here's hoping Hempstead comes thru...

The flavor of time and 5 card stud...

From the last letter I sent Bone thru you, you now have some idea of my new situation here on this island. Yes, and although the game is not over by a long-shot, it's nice to feel as if I've got a winning hand after looking at kangaroo flushes for so long... A card was received along with your letter on Friday when the boat arrived. My associates were reassuring me of the leaf harvest down in Morocco... Looks as if this madness is proceeding rather well and in a few weeks, *Inshallah*, preparations for Central Park Canoe Race should be completed...

At the moment I'm crossed-legged in lotus just at the edge of a sloping hill above the sea...the sun isn't up yet but the birds are stirring and the soft breeze that precedes the dawn is riffling this paper... Some fishing boats are bobbing at anchor about a mile off shore... They'll be working the waters around the island this day then back to Istanbul or some other mainland city in the evening... Huge gray Cumulonimbus clouds ride the horizon like some great fleet gathering on the Asian shore... Their flanks are tingeing pink and pearl as the sun slowly climbs the sky... Chickens crawing out their raggedy songs and a quick flash of T. Jay's barnyard waking up one morning in Virginia...

What's happened to Schock? I mean, is he even around anymore in word or deed... No news for years now... Is he dead or just off somewhere preparing some fiendish madness to spring upon an unsuspecting world?

The flies are nibbling my ankles so I'll quit for a while. Barbara wrote me yesterday that she's trying to make contact with you. I realize you may have differing views of her but the lady's been my eyes while I'm in here and our souls are mingled... Love her for my sake...

6:45

A short word about the food. I just have to tell you about breakfast this morning. I mean, sheep-brain-soup. Can you fucking believe that!? Usually it's some sort of watery broth for breakfast, then at noon and dinner we alternate between two different kinds of beans and rice or macaroni... They all smell the same an hour later when everyone begins farting...The room where I sleep has a curious sort of cloud floating near the high grimy ceiling... Flies and mosquito have learned not to venture too near, they drop dead like a stone if they enter that floating fartwind...

If I stop I can get this out on a boat today with a friend who's going free. So write me and I'll be on touch soon. Sun rising in many ways. Which way to the bulls?

Love,
Billy

8-15-75, Friday
Imrali

Barb,

So much to say and describe and feelings to relate that I really find it hard to begin…received your postcard and then that fine fine letter. And letters from my father and brother after your visit. Yes, I knew what it would mean to them all to speak with you. I'm happy they're happy. You've touched them and it's good for all of us, this contact, this touching…

If you've read my letter to them then I can dispense with some of the physical descriptions and maybe just send a few pieces from my notebook:

Naked and alone, wandering the beach at the far end of the island… Only prisoners here on this island, no people around or allowed… So fine to swim without clothes then walk the shoreline, light and free, my cock bouncing jauntily in the breeze…

In underwear and sneakers I climb a high sloping ridge and rocky cliff at the very end of the N.E. point…high up where the gulls roost, their raunching calls blown past me by the steady gusting wind…very high it is, almost more than I bargain for…and some tense moments of doubt and a frightening slip when my face pushes into a crevice and instead of the relief I expect to find, a sticky spider's web and a huge white brown spider right over my mouth… I let loose both hands in sudden panic but just manage to grab some roots as I begin sliding backwards over the edge…

The setting sun extends itself straight across the water from a lavender horizon in a glittering line to my eye as I sit here on the beach in lotus in love with the world… A huge chalk moon hanging above the cliffs behind me… Flies rise off the sand to settle on my naked body as the sinking sun settles on the sea… The mass of cliffs to my right are darkening now, these same cliffs I climbed and almost died on yesterday morning…darkening against the dusky horizon so that the gulls fly out off it like specks of life off some great living thing, like specks of thought flying out off the edge of this paper, the edge of this sea, the edge of this mind I realize with, fantasize with… And now the sun just an apricot taste on the purple sky, a narrow band of flavored light on the water that laps so gently now at my feet, as the wind has settled and rested behind the great coming stillness of the moon…

I'm between the setting sun and the rising moon, between years of life that was prison and a new life that will begin (or continue is better) when I'm free… And I'm sitting on the beach from which I hope to follow the sun…

And last week I'm lying up there on my bed in the evening with my arms back behind my head when this throw-back from the next bunk he says, "Whyn't you shave your hair, it's dirty…?" I ask him "What?" and he says "This hair," as he leans across to pluck out a few from my right armpit.

"Shit," I yell and smack his hand away. "You fucking crazy?!"

"You should shave this, it's *pis*, not clean," he says to me, this orc who's been working and eating and sleeping all in the same clothes every day since I got here and who knows how long before that.

I say, "Look, whose hair is it, mine or yours?"

"But you should shave, its'…"

"Yeah, I know, it's dirty and full of bug eggs but you take care of your pits and I'll take care of mine. Now leave me in peace to write a letter…"

So he just sits quiet for a while, just stares at me while I write. I'm used to the stares. Then he reaches down, takes hold of the crotch of his pyjamas and says to me, "You *sunnet*, circumsized?"

"Shit, yes, I'm circumcised, you want to see?"

And he does, which is why he asked, so I just put in my Air Force earplugs and turn the other way to finish the letter…

Sitting on the lighthouse atop one end of the horse-shoe bay… The sea a hundred feet beneath me, clear translucent in the last rays of the afternoon sun and the whole Marmara stretched out flat calm before me…

The wind's been heavy for days now with great swells crashing against the fishing boats that tried to run them… Now the wind has dropped and the sea is a glaze over which quick-scudding V's of geese glide, and slow wheeling gulls craw across in lazy-winged flight…the insect hum off the yellowed grass and so so many birds singing, flickering the sky to take the last rays of the sinking sun on their wings… There's a ship down here off the edge of the cliffs that forms the cove…sounds echo and carry…the eerie metal creaking of its winch rises and falls among the gullcry, like an animal in pain it sounds, so small down there working on the bobbing sea…

Me, just a stone among the other stones, resting here at this height, at the edge of the island, so aware, so aware of the sea…

Barb, so many things to say to you. Yesterday I sat in the shade beneath some trees eating fresh figs I picked myself, and all the while your presence so strong around me, within me. And August 8th, all those tumbling eights so many years ago now…

I feel life singing thru me now, words like the wind and a rhythm of the sea. I long to wrap you in the arms of my song. I feel you singing within me, so strong and clear and full of light…

I'll send this out on the boat today. Write me some details about time and place. When do you expect to be back in Europe? If it's not for a few months, perhaps we can spend a quiet evening in a small seafood restaurant I used to know back on Long Island. Otherwise, I need your European address. Yes, for sure this time…

Soon babe,

I love you,

Billy

8-20-75. Wednesday

Folks,

Yes, a huge orange moon rising above the mountains on the Asian coast across the sea from where I sit on this soft August evening...

Dad, your latest (12th) letter arrived yesterday. I was sorry to hear you hadn't received my letter of August 5th but I guess you've gotten it by now. This communication gap is a bit much. And I also haven't heard from Mike. He did say he'd write and I'm sure he will but the current state of Turko-American politics doesn't lend itself toward fulfillment of the trade-deal, so I guess he's waiting for something positive to write about. It appears to me that it's getting sort of late in the season for any trades to be made, what with the world series coming up soon. And this is world series time, that's for sure...

I had to pull another tooth last Friday. At least it won't pain me anymore. Got a letter from Dave Bloch at the Consulate. He says he'll be out here Sept. 5th with an American Army dentist to give my teeth a thorough check. They better hurry. At the way they're dropping, there won't be anything to look at if they're not quick. I'm at the point where my teeth just aren't so important anymore. Yeah, I know, brush after meals and all that, but 5 years without any real dental care has taken its toll. I'm beginning to think it's supernatural. That I'm possessed by Turkish demons. They can't get at my mind because it's just too far out to reach, so they strike at the weakest point in my body—i.e. the toothes...Out! Out!! damn spirits...in the name of Colgate, Stripe, and Ipana I banish you back to the nether worlds of Pain Creatures...

Ahem, yes, anyway, Dave also said it was O.K. to send that package I mentioned in my last letter to the Consulate in his name.

How did it turn out calling that T. woman in xxxxx? I hope it's not a big hassle. Her husband (ex-husband, out of necessity since he's been in jail 12 years on a 24 year sentence reduced from life for a little murder) he's a good friend of mine here. It's strange how many of my friends are killers. Weird world I live in here.

I couldn't swim for about a week because of my tooth but after the dentist pulled it last Friday, I've been in the water every day since. Actually am working on a nice tan. Will wonders ever cease?

Mom, I hear you're into bike riding now. Just remember what I said about getting too far from home. You do have navigation problems. Even in a car. Maybe it's better if you just go around the block. It'll be hard to get lost like that. But seriously, keep riding, it's really good exercise. I wish I could join you for some morning rides. I want to ride a nice ten-speed all over the U.S. Maybe we could split and make it out to California together.

Thursday nite

Been hefting these 50 kilos sacks of beans all day today and am really tired. But I feel good. Even was swimming for almost the entire 12-2 lunch break and then lifting more beans all afternoon. I've got a nice tan and my arms are like steel. But I must say this working-man's life just doesn't seem to be where I'm at. It's good after the stagnation of Bayrampasha but I think I'm made for different things… Yes, well, that's most probably what the guy said up on the scaffold…

There are so many dogs and cats here on the island… I play with these 3 little black and white puppies who are always outside the *kogus*, sniffing around early in the morning…

Yesterday I was up in a tree back up in the hills behind our little village… A fig tree no less…so so fine to climb a tree and eat fresh fruit while the wind rustles the leaves and gulls craw across the sky…I felt like some albino monkey up there sniffing the breezes and scoffing down those figs…

I take it Peggy's going back to school soon so the shopping season is in full swing… And Peg, seeing as how you're in your 2d year of college now I think it only right to expect a letter. I mean, you do write them now and then so how about some kind of informative letter letting me know the whereabouts of your head. I mean, what are you into? Reading books? What books? Did you ever get into Hatha Yoga? You should, it's the best thing possible for health and body. A bit difficult perhaps at the beginning but once you're into it you'll never stop. And mediation? Hmmm...

Anyway, write and perhaps a photo or two and don't be surprised if I show up in Boston one of these days. Is there a social stigma attached to having a dangerous criminal for a brother? Or a son? That side of the issue is hard on you people, perhaps. I'm sorry if it is but for me the problem doesn't exist and certainly won't exist when I'm free. I could almost care after all this time.

Well, I guess I'll finish and seal this up. Will send it off with one of the visitors who'll come here tomorrow on the boat. I may even have one or two. Who knows?

There isn't anything to say about transfer to N.Y. news until you see Mike again. I'll wait to hear what he says but I'm sure I already know. I've heard it before in one form or another.

Barb likes all of you as much as you like her. I'm glad. It's been a link for all of us. Brings us closer, this personal contact.

O.K., leaning a bit off third and if the pitcher goes into a full wind-up, well, we'll see about Willie Mays' move... Don't sweat it, though, not about to pick up a tag now...

I think I'll get a letter from you tomorrow with the boat so maybe there'll be time for some additional below...

Love, laughs
Billy

Thursday
Sept. 18th
75

Folks,

Yes, I know, it's been a while since you've heard from me. Many reasons for not writing. All poor excuses. I'm sorry, I love you people very much and forgive me for hurting you.

That news about Harriet James' letter rather upset me. Not so much in what she said but that she said it. I don't want you to worry more than you already do so or her to scare you with this business annoys me to no end.

Yes, I know all about patience and Mike's efforts and the negotiations in Ankara. I've known about them for 2 years now. Sorry, but I have to go my own way. It's just been too long. If good news comes down from Ankara then fine, I'll go along. It's O.K. with me if they take me back to N.Y. (Even though I don't intend to spend any time or probation there). . . . But I'm just going ahead with my own plans. . . . I don't really expect you to understand this . . . You'd have to spend 5 years your life locked up to understand it . . . But when you write of 'soon having 2 years them counting down from the last year then free' well, I just totally reject this view . . .

9-18-75, Thursday

Folks,

Yes, I know, it's been a while since you've heard from me. Many reasons for not writing. All poor excuses. I'm sorry, I love you people very much and forgive me for hurting you.

That news about Harriet James' letter rather upset me *[Dear Harriet James came for a visit and sussed out that I wasn't planning to spend the winter on this island, and fearing for my safety, wrote to my folks, upsetting them]*. Not so much in what she said but that she said it. I don't want you to worry more than you already do, so for her to scare you with this business annoys me to no end. Yes, I know all about patience and Mike's efforts and the negotiations in Ankara. I've known about them for 2 years now. Sorry, but I have to go my own way. It's just been too long. If good news comes down from Ankara then fine, I'll go along. It's O.K. with me if they take me back to N.Y. (even though I don't intend to spend any time on probation there)... But I'm just going ahead with my own plan... I don't really expect you to understand this... You'd have to spend 5 years of your life locked up to understand it... But when you write of "soon having 2 years then counting down from the last year then free", well, I just totally reject this view...

The situation is that I lack essential ingredients, without which I cannot act. As I've said before, I won't come off the bag unless I'm sure of reaching the plate. Problem is that I can't get outside coordination. So I bide my time waiting for the ingredients and wondering what's happening in Ankara with these papers Mike is supposed to have sent.

Actually the situation is such a piece of pie if only a craft were available. Anyway, let us see what comes down in the coming days. I'm really becoming disenchanted with this Island. The work is bad enough but to live 24 hours a day with these natives is becoming unbearable.

I haven't heard from your people since the August 29th letter. Mail is here today but won't be given out until tonight, after this letter is sent. So any reply to your letter will have to wait until next week to go out. I'm assuming there's a letter from you there. None last week but what with McBee's wedding I expect there's some news. You've gotten my last letter with the package go-ahead but I don't know how it will get here due to a closing of A.P.O. privileges by the Turks due to the political situation. Again, will have to wait and see.

I'm doing all right, but am really sort of lonely here. The people around me are not the sort of people I find much common ground with. If it weren't for the baseballish advantages I would prefer Bayrampasha now that winter is coming. I don't plan on being here this winter but through what set of circumstances this is effected, I just can't say at the moment. My outside coordinators *[Joey, who was free, in Turkey, had visited me, had my money for a boat...and disappeared]* have been silent this past month. I'm anxious for word from them. If they'd come across, then I could cross the plate, showering in the locker room before the other team even knows the game is over.

There obviously hasn't been any news out of Ankara or I would have heard from either you or the Consul. My feelings are that this newest initiative by Mike et al will just be washed away with the others. The Turk-Am political climate is cloudy indeed. A favor will be hard to get at this point.

I'm having a hard time composing my thoughts so I'll end this letter. I keep postponing writing hoping to make a phone call (collect, of course) instead. Perhaps one of these late nights we'll have a chat...who knows...

Don't worry, things will work out for the best...

Love,

Billy

Sept. 28th
'75

Dad

Don't know as this may be the last letter I'll be writing to you. I'm waiting daily for the aligning of certain weather factors which will finalize the plan I've decided to act upon. I'll explain a little better. . . . There are as usual, as we've discussed before, advantages to keeping as many trains running at the same time as we possibly can . . . . Coming down the middle track, at an indeterminable speed, is that 2-year running Transfer-Train . . . Yes, and this is moving into the 4th week since an answer was expected from our contacted official. In all honesty you must admit that these expected answers to our queries have a tendency to drag on for months. . . which would be O.K. if we knew for certain the correct response was forthcoming from the T. govt. . . . which we don't . . . Consider the past circumstances that just always somehow throw this train off the track . . . I mean 2 years it's chugging, uphill but still chugging and maybe, maybe. . . it's going to get home one of these fine days. . . O. Inshallah . . . . But now there's that train that I've been watching here on the far outside-track which just can't be kept running very

9-28-75

Dad,

Don't know as if this may be the last letter I'll be writing to you. I'm waiting daily for the aligning of certain weather factors which will finalize the plan I've decided to act upon. I'll explain a little better... There are, as usual, as we've discussed before, advantages to keeping as many trains running at the same time as we possibly can... Coming down the middle track, at an indeterminable speed, is that 2-year running Transfer-train... Yes, and this is moving into the 4th week since an answer was expected from our "contacted official". In all honesty you must admit that these expected answers to our queries have a tendency to drag on for months... Which would be O.K. if we knew for certain the correct response was forthcoming from the T. govt....which we don't... Consider the past circumstances that just always somehow throw this train off the track... I mean 2 years it's chugging, uphill but still chugging and maybe, maybe...it's going to get home one of these fine days... *Inshallah*... But now there's that train that I've been watching here on the far-outside-track which just can't be kept running very much longer before it gets bogged down by the cold winter weather... And Spring is just too long away after 5 years... I know you'll find it difficult to appreciate and will surely disagree with the logic of a sure three versus a possible 13... And with the transfer reply, note the "reply", not the transfer, seemingly so close now, I realize you would say waiting is the more correct choice of action, or non-action, if you will... But now we're back to the weather factors, and the next correct alignment, I open the throttle on my Ghost-train, that ole Midnight Express, and drift on down the line... The possibility of a derailment exists only as one of several possibility-tracks and the other lines are clear freighting all the way... I like it, I'm going to engineer my way right on thru this bullshit and clear the streams of our lives of this clotting... Again I say that you'll find it hard to agree with the logic... And do not think I haven't considered the anguish of loved ones hurt in the derailment... I have, for 2 years and more the consideration of this has stayed me from riding an impulse into what might or might not have been a 'foolish move'... But do not think that I consider this a foolish move... It is certainly a more dangerous train to ride than the Transfer Special but it has the advantage of speed... It immediately gets you to your destination... And although you would have to be 5 years held against your will to appreciate it, I'm sure you'll understand when I say that I've just got to move... Just have to get on this train because it's heading in my direction and I feel it's right on schedule with the rhythm of my lifebeat... Got to get on to where I'm going if I want to be me... Just, simply, got to...

There's not too much more to say... I know you won't agree and the logic can only be truly appreciated seen from the end of a 5 year telescope, but I'm sure you'll all love the result as much as I will because I'm going to make it work...

Tonight is Sunday... This letter will be sent from here Tuesday and posted by Wednesday... You won't get it until the following Monday, I suppose...and I think weather conditions will align before then... So if you get a telephone call before this letter arrives, disregard the entire above... It'll be from me, *Inshallah*...

If you haven't heard anything one way or the other then just sit tight and news of a kind will be definitely forthcoming... I'm thinking it will be before the Ankara News but if not, fine, I'm for cruising out in style...

Don't fret or write any entreating letters... Certainly don't pull a Harriet and begin contacting in panic... I'm at the station waiting like you... Let's ride the train that arrives...

Love to you Mom and Dad and everyone...

Pray as you each know how... I am...

Billy

AFTERWORD

Four days later, on a stormy night, I escaped off Imrali Island in a rowboat. I ran through Turkey for three days, swam across the Maritsa River into Greece, and was arrested and held for nearly two weeks at a remote border post in the woods. Five days after my escape, and two days before my last letter arrived, my parents received a phone call from the American Consul informing them that I was missing and a rowboat had been found on the Asia Minor coastline. It was about a week more before my parents learned that I was alive and free. The Greeks graciously deported me as being "a bad influence upon the youth of Greece"—the same charge brought against Socrates. After a few days in Amsterdam, I returned home on October 24, 1975 and embraced my father at Kennedy Airport, before turning to face a mob of reporters with lights, cameras, and shouted questions; but that's another story...

ABOUT THE AUTHOR

Billy Hayes has been writing, speaking, acting, and directing in theater, film, and television since his escape in 1975. He lives with his wife, Wendy, in Los Angeles, still practices yoga daily, and appreciates every sweet, magical moment.

For more information, please go to www.billyhayes.com.